The Contemporary Christian Music Debate

THE CONTEMPORARY CHRISTIAN MUSIC DEBATE

STEVE MILLER

Tyndale House Publishers, Inc.
Wheaton, Illinois

Library of Congress Cataloging-in-Publication Data

Miller, Steve, 1957-
   The contemporary Christian music debate : worldly compromise or agent of renewal? / Steve Miller.
     p. cm.
  Includes bibliographical references.
  ISBN 0-8423-1230-7
  1. Contemporary Christian music—History and criticism.
I. Title.
ML3187.5.M54   1993
246'.7—dc20   92-30629

Printed in the United States of America

00 99 98 97 96 95 94 93
8   7   6   5   4   3   2   1

Contents

PREFACE

For me it all began in 1974 when my Bible-study teacher persuaded me to attend a Christian concert. Half expecting something resembling a church choir, I was overwhelmed by the excitement generated by a band that used a popular style to communicate spiritual truth.

I enjoyed the music, was drawn into worship with the sing-alongs, was motivated to make Jesus my first love, and took home the first of many contemporary Christian albums so that I could experience the same impact in the privacy of my home. In fact, the albums and tapes proved so beneficial to the renewing of my mind that Christian groups such as Love Song, Truth, and Maranatha soon replaced Led Zeppelin, the Stones, and other secular bands who cared nothing for my spiritual welfare.

Those were exciting days—days of witnessing on the streets, studying the Word, and seeing the lives of friends transformed by the power of the gospel. And the fruit remained—some friends landing on the mission field and many others faithfully serving local churches, even to this day.

Perhaps it was, in part, our youthfulness that later caused me to question the music that had become so central to the movement. Men of God under whom I sat, men who were older and by far wiser than I, dogmatically asserted that this new church music was a subtle form of compromise, a wolf in sheep's clothing designed by the enemy to infiltrate the church with the world. Now I was a sheep, but I had no intention of having the wool pulled over my eyes. As for compromise, I wanted nothing to do with it.

These men claimed that psychological studies had proven that contemporary styles weakened the physical body, promoted sensuality, and contained a beat used in primitive cultures for demonic worship. I was stunned. Could it be that they were right, and I had been deceived? I asked God for discernment, but my prayers yielded no inner caution from the Spirit. Yet I knew of others who had been sincere on issues, yet—biblically—they were sincerely wrong.

I decided that my only option was to prayerfully study both sides of the issue. But resources were scarce. Those that were available either failed to deal with major criticisms or fell short in their documentation. So, after exhausting the current literature, I moved on to primary research. I traced the history of our hymns, waded through every relevant psychological study I could find, and interviewed those who had utilized contemporary Christian music over the years.

The aim of my research was not to prove a point or set people straight. I just wanted to get at the facts and to follow wherever they led. Jesus was Lord over my music, and I determined that if I found Gregorian chant to be God's exclusive style of music, I would burn all else and acquire a taste.

In the early stages it was never my intention to write a book, but after my search drew to a close, my experiences in subsequent years of ministry proved that I was far from alone in my struggles over this issue. On every hand parents, educators, and church leaders were having to chart their course in a land of few signposts and many contradictory maps. So to these fellow pilgrims I present the results of my labors in hopes that, even if you disagree with my conclusions, you will at least better understand the issues involved and be more fully equipped to chart your own course.

To reap the greatest benefit from the following pages, consider these suggestions.

First, strive for objectivity. Music and worship forms are emotionally charged issues that strongly resist rational analysis. Thus, discussions often generate more heat than light. If you find that your reasons for reading are more to stock your arsenal and beef up your position than to humbly seek God's face, please stop reading, close the book, and pray a simple prayer for objectivity and guidance. Here is a brief prayer that has expressed the desire of my heart as I have researched this book:

> *Dear Lord, You know that I come to this study with preconceived ideas, attitudes, and opinions. As sincerely as I hold my position, I shudder to realize that many sincere individuals have been sincerely wrong. Please grant me wisdom from on high and the ruthless objectivity that will allow me to drop my cherished*

beliefs should they conflict with your eternal truth.

Second, prepare yourself for a mental challenge. I take the objections raised by critics very seriously and believe that each one deserves a thoughtful response. This book seeks to bring order to the many issues involved, and the sources have been carefully documented. Part One examines objections that have been leveled at contemporary Christian music; Part Two searches the Scriptures for God's perspective on music and worship; Part Three views the present controversy from the fascinating, and often entertaining, perspective of the history of our hymns; Part Four moves from the defensive posture to an urgent plea for using contemporary Christian music.

I commend you for taking seriously one of the most compelling issues faced by today's church. My prayer is that this book will promote healing in a divided church and open doors for presenting Jesus clearly to a lost and dying world.

ACKNOWLEDGMENTS

As I began this study, little did I know that I was embarking upon a journey. Sometimes the path led me through familiar territories. Often, though, I found myself in fields that were unfamiliar or even on paths that were apparently uncharted. At these points I dared not travel alone, so I sought out guides who felt quite at home in these unfamiliar areas. At yet other legs of the journey, I needed the input of friends and family. Truly, "through presumption comes nothing but strife, but with those who receive counsel is wisdom" (Prov. 13:10), and to these counselors I wish to express my gratitude.

To the professors and church leaders who offered their invaluable critiques: Dr. J. Robertson McQuilkin, chancellor of Columbia Bible College and Seminary, for his theological insights; G. William Supplee, former professor of music and Dr. David C. Osterlund, chairman of the music department at C.B.C.S., for their insights on music and missions; Dr. Henry Virkler, professor of psychology and counseling at Liberty University, for his insights on psychology; Dr. Carl Wilson, for reading the history chapters and offering suggestions; Josh McDowell and Dr. Bill Jones, who encouraged me and lobbied for a more popular style; and Rev. Jim Burgess, for his pastoral perspective.

To all the family and friends who offered their insights and encouragement along the way: my mother, Ann Miller, who read through the manuscript at several stages, spotting typos, correcting

grammar, and offering suggestions; my father, Joe
Miller, for his wise counsel; my wife, Laurene, for
her special insights and support; my brothers,
Philip and Richard, and their wives, Marilyn and
Angela; Laurene's parents, Howard and Annie
Laura; Betty Sue and Fornadia Cook; Bryan McIn-
tosh, Jeff Stark, Jamie Hammock, Michael Bentley,
and Erin Butterworth, for research assistance on a
couple of occasions; and Harold Baker, John Joyce,
Ken Walker, Tim Gunter, Delana Duckworth, Jeri
Bruner, Rhoda Barge, and David and Judy Hadden,
for reading and offering suggestions.

To my fellow ministers, pastor Bill Priester and
minister of music Scott Davis, for their wonderful
spirit as we have dealt with these issues in day-to-
day ministry.

To all my new friends at Tyndale House, who
have made the publishing process a joy.

1

The Christian Music Controversy

After years of research, I have reached this conclusion: Contemporary Christian music is a medium whose day has come for families, churches, evangelists, and, to an increasingly greater extent, foreign missionaries. Yet the hesitancy of the church to release the full potential of this tool demonstrates that many unanswered questions still plague the minds of believers. In addition, a heated debate continues to rage among Christian leaders.

Hailed by some as a fresh moving of the Holy Spirit, maligned by others as blatant compromise with the world, contemporary Christian music has become one of the most controversial issues facing the church at the close of the twentieth century.

The widespread use and apparent impact of this medium demands that the early opponents—who scoffed at "Jesus Music" in the late sixties and early seventies, brushing it off as a passing fad—should take a second look at music that has become a major vehicle of both evangelism and dis-

cipleship. Christian bookstores carry a full line of
recordings, from children's tapes with a contemporary beat to the Christian rock of Petra and
DeGarmo and Key and the mellow soft rock of
Sandi Patti. Christian radio carries the music into
autos and homes. Accompaniment tapes and youth
musicals take this music from individual use into
the church.

Some rapidly growing churches, particularly
those targeting baby boomers, incorporate contemporary choruses and music specials with a pop
sound as the main course for their worship.[1]
Church growth experts are taking note of the connection between styles of worship and church
growth. James Emery White, leadership consultant
for preaching and worship within the Southern Baptist Convention, observes that "perhaps one of the
most clearly observed marks of many fast-growing
churches is their shift away from traditional hymnody toward contemporary music."[2] Award-win-
ning journalist Russell Chandler observes that these
new styles of worship are "making an indelible
imprint upon the way many churches integrate
music and worship."[3]

Considered radical in its early years, contemporary Christian music has since been embraced by
many respected Christian leaders and has recorded
some remarkable accomplishments. Chuck Smith,
innovative pastor of Calvary Chapel in Costa
Mesa, California, reaped the fruit of the Jesus
Movement and reported five thousand people were

saved in one year through his church's concert ministry.[4] Josh McDowell, who through his books and extensive speaking has become one of America's premier defenders of the Christian faith, has teamed up with a contemporary Christian rock group, Petra (transliteration of the Greek word for "rock"), to pack out auditoriums all over the United States. There they challenge teenagers to receive the timeless message of the gospel and radically follow Jesus. Billy Graham has allowed such Christian pop singers as Kenny Marks and Cliff Richard to share his crusade platform.

This movement shows no signs of abating. Chandler predicts that the trend toward using contemporary forms in the local church's worship will "play fortissimo beyond 2001, especially as new songbooks, lyrics, and Christian artists gain attention."[5]

Still, though this trend is "the greatest revolution in the modern church," according to church growth specialist Elmer Towns, it "is also the source of the greatest controversy."[6] Opponents amass evidence to show that what, on the surface, appears to be a useful, even God-sent tool is actually a thinly veiled device of the Enemy. They maintain that the church's embrace of this tool merely demonstrates the appeal of the world to the flesh and the lack of discernment by the church at large. Opponents insist that the fruit being produced through this medium will not last and, at best, will have a worm in it.

In fact, the compromise is considered so serious and widespread that one author concludes: "I view this integration of rock music and the worship of God as clear evidence that the church has entered the final Laodicean age of apostasy."[7] This strong contention exemplifies the intense feelings on both sides of the controversy. The lines have been drawn, but the answer still is not clear. Is this music of the devil or of God, bane or blessing, worldly or godly?

The contentions are many and varied, and proceed not only from the vantage point of theology but also from the domains of church history, psychology, scientific studies, music theory, aesthetics, anthropology, and missionary strategy. The missionary strategist must determine whether accommodation to the musical tastes of other cultures is biblical compromise or simply wise mission strategy. The college president or trustee must decide whether or not to offer training in contemporary worship forms. Church staff members must give direction to congregations that are often divided over musical tastes and convictions. Parents must decide whether or not Christian rock is a viable alternative to secular rock for their children.

Perhaps because of the cross-disciplinary nature of the study of music in the church (many pastors have no musical background; many musicians lack a theological background) and the intensity of the conflict, most Christians would rather avoid the conflict than tackle the issues. But where avoidance may be tolerated and even considered wise on lesser issues (for example, should we change the color of the carpet in the vestibule?), most of us have not been afforded this luxury regarding contemporary music. The controversy rages on many fronts, and there seems to be no safe middle ground on which to stand.

In the following pages you will find discussions of the essential questions that all of us must answer:

- Have scientists proven that rock music harms both mind and body?
- Does contemporary music use the same kind of beat used by African tribes to call upon demons?
- Do contemporary music styles lead to moral corruption?
- Do we compromise when we take something from the world and use it for God?
- What does the Bible say about music and styles of worship?
- What can we learn from the history of our hymns?
- How can parents talk to their children about their music?
- How can churches use contemporary Christian music without alienating those who object?
- Is there a place for contemporary Christian music in missions?
- How are growing churches using contemporary forms in worship?

Most people have opinions on these matters, yet

few have developed convictions through sincere prayer, biblical studies, and solid research. This book has been written to clarify muddy waters and to provide a perspective that will better equip you to make your own choices.

PART ONE

CONTEMPORARY CHRISTIAN MUSIC UNDER FIRE

2

CHARGES OF HEALTH THREATS

The purpose of psychology is to give us a com-
pletely different idea of the things we know best.
                                              Paul Valery

Perhaps the most devastating attack on contemporary music has been launched from the field of psychology. My first exposure to this line of reasoning
was at a seminar that I attended as a youth. The
teacher dogmatically asserted that the rock beat
was harmful to both mind and body, backing his
contention with the studies of New York psychiatrist John Diamond. These studies figure promi-
nently in anti-rock literature[1] and demand a careful
evaluation.

JOHN DIAMOND'S BEHAVIORAL KINESIOLOGY

In a nutshell, Dr. Diamond exposes subjects to various stimuli and measures their muscular strength to
determine the effect of the stimuli on the body.[2] He
tests a subject's strength by first having him extend
his arm to his side, parallel to the floor. The tester

pushes down on the arm, examining the bounce and spring. The subject should be able to resist the pressure.

The next step is to introduce a variable that Diamond claims weakens the body. For example, the tester would put a piece of plastic on top of the subject's head or have him think of an unpleasant situation. "In nearly every case," according to Diamond, "the subject will be unable to resist the pressure."[3]

Diamond believes that many of the stimuli to which we are exposed every day—including certain forms of music—sap our energy and diminish our quality of life. Diamond calls this branch of research "behavioral kinesiology."

Concerning music, he claims that a person's muscle strength is reduced by approximately two-thirds when music containing a certain beat is introduced. The damaging beat, he claims, is one that goes da-da-DA (known in poetry as an *anapestic* beat), the opposite of the waltzlike DA-da-da. Though not all contemporary music has this beat, a large proportion of it does. (The old "Rock and Roll" music of the Beatles, for example, did not, but the newer "Rock," such as Glen Campbell's "Southern Nights," does.) Songs containing this beat are now well represented in the Top Ten of any given week. Interestingly enough, Diamond asserts that volume makes no difference—the weakening effect is evident at any level. The style can be hard rock or soft; it doesn't matter. It is the *pattern* of the beat that is the supposed problem.[4]

Obviously this line of argument, if correct, is devastating to the contemporary Christian music enterprise. Even mellow rock music, which appeals to most adults, cannot evade the critique of Dr. Diamond's behavioral kinesiology. According to this theory, as sincere as the musicians and producers may be, contemporary Christian music is harming many people. It matters not how godly the musicians or how theologically accurate the lyrics may be. Neither does it matter whether we are speaking of the harder rock of Petra or the softer music of Sandi Patti; the problem is in the music itself. If Dr. Diamond is correct, contemporary Christian music is damaging or even destroying lives. But is he right?

Having carefully evaluated Diamond's methods and conclusions, I would like to forward the following observations, which raise serious questions about the accuracy of his findings.

First, the tests he has used to evaluate contemporary music, if valid, have ramifications beyond music—ramifications most people would find unacceptable. If we accept Dr. Diamond's conclusions on rock music, we would seem obligated to apply his unique methodology in other areas.

Diamond asserts that not only does the rock beat cause weakness, but so does reading silently, rubbing one's nose, listening on the phone without alternating ears, weight lifting with both arms at the same time, looking at a frowning face, wearing clothes made of synthetic material (such as polyester, acrylic, and nylon), and listening to the note C.[5]

To truly accept Diamond's conclusions, critics of the rock beat would need to restrict much more than their music.

Although this argument in itself is not fatal to Diamond's hypothesis—it is not impossible that these practices have ill effects hitherto unknown to us—these findings do seem odd and beckon us to take a closer look at all of Diamond's theories.

Second, practical experience undercuts Dr. Diamond's conclusions. If he were right, people who work out at health spas (which generally play popular music in the background) would be suddenly sapped of approximately two-thirds of their body strength when songs with "the beat" came through the sound system. Thus, a person working out with 180 pounds on the bench press would suddenly drop the weight, being able to lift only 60 pounds. The proposition that certain rock songs dramatically and immediately weaken muscles is invalidated by thousands of weight lifters worldwide every day.

In fact, a record of thirty-five thousand sit-ups was recently set by Timothy Kides, a Glassboro State College sophomore, "with rock music booming from a portable radio."[6] Apparently, his strength was not overly sapped by the music! Thus, observations from our daily experience call Dr. Diamond's findings into question.

Third, Diamond's conclusions are contradicted by many other psychological studies. Since a biased researcher could uncover scientific studies from somewhere to support most any opinion, a more thorough study of the extant literature is in order. I studied all of the relevant psychological literature I could find that was published from the early 1960s to the present. This study yielded many insights on the psychological effects of musical styles. (Note: Although I am using Dr. Diamond's assertions as a starting point, the following study will apply equally to other assertions that popular music styles cause psychological harm.)

MUSIC AND TASK PERFORMANCE

Dr. Diamond concludes that rock music causes a loss of energy and posits that work inefficiency will result (for example, decreased output and more errors).[7] Yet other studies have yielded the opposite result. A 1979 North Carolina State study[8] began by noting the established fact that, in practical tasks such as long-term driving, monitoring radar-scopes, and industrial inspection, people's vigilance (alertness, watchfulness, attentiveness) decreases over a period of time, resulting in an increase in the probability of errors. The object of the N.C. State study was to ascertain what effect music might have on the maintenance of vigilance.

A summary of the test was stated as follows: The subjects "performed a vigilance task under familiar rock, familiar easy listening, unfamiliar rock, unfamiliar easy listening, and no music conditions." The result? "Familiar music significantly increased heart rate and percent detections, and also helped subjects maintain vigilance over a period of time, thus decreasing the probability of errors. *Type of music had no significant effect.*"[9]

The results of this test contradict Diamond's hypothesis. Familiar music, regardless of style, actually heightened awareness and thus improved performance.

A 1988 University of Kentucky experiment also contradicted Diamond's assertion. Ninety-six subjects were assigned to one of four experimental groups in an effort to test the effect of background music on their ability to perform 220 eye/hand coordination problems. The four groups were: task only, task and classical background music, task and jazz background music, and task and popular background music. The popular piece was "We Don't Need Another Hero," the Tina Turner theme song from the movie *Mad Max Beyond Thunderdome.*

The four conditions made no significant difference in the number of problems completed (that is, the ability to perform the task). Yet, it is interesting to note that thirty-four students reported that they *felt* the music interfered with their performance. Eight felt distracted by the popular piece, twelve by the classical, and fourteen by the jazz.

I am not concluding that classical music is therefore more distracting than rock; other factors such as preferences and familiarity would need to be controlled to test such a hypothesis. The primary conclusion of this study was that "the experimental condition had no significant effect on task performance."[10]

A 1989 University of Illinois study found subjects generally performing better on tests when familiar, popular music was played in the background rather than less-familiar classical music.[11]

Still, critics of the rock beat claim that a 1987 study with mice presents contrary evidence to the aforementioned university studies. According to these critics, "constant exposure to a heavy rock beat caused mice to lose learning and memory capabilities," and actually altered the brain tissue of the mice.[12] However, an examination of the study reveals that the mice were never exposed to a rock beat. The experiment was not designed to compare the effects of different rhythms. Rather, they compared the effects of classical rhythms with the effects of nonrhythmic beats (chaotic drumbeats that were out of synch with any dominant beat). Rock music was neither used nor even mentioned in the study.[13]

The error apparently originated when *Insight* magazine incorrectly reported that the experiment compared the effects of "different musical rhythms." (Since *rhythm* is by definition a regular pattern, the chaotic beats of this experiment should neither be designated as rhythms nor be equated with rock beats, which are actual rhythms.) The magazine then linked the detrimental sounds with the rock beat.[14]

Finally, the critics quoted the magazine apparently without reading the original study and assumed that the experimenters used a rock beat. They used nothing of the sort.[15] The resulting confusion has been unfortunate.

A study published in the *Indian Journal of Applied Psychology* did compare the effects of rock and classical music on albino rats. It was found in this study that both styles of music aided the learning process in the early stages and hindered it in the latter stages. Further, both styles helped the rats to maintain their learned response after they had been exposed to stress.[16]

But the studies using human subjects are much more important in this regard, not only because of our psychological distance from rats but also because of our ability to account for such variables as familiarity and preference.

What we can conclude from this section is that rock music has not been shown, in and of itself, to inhibit performance. In fact, if the rock songs are familiar to the subjects, they may very well enhance performance in certain circumstances.

MUSIC AND STRESS REDUCTION

Recent studies on music and stress reduction also impact our present discussion, particularly since some claim that rock irritates the listener and produces stress.

In a 1984 Pennsylvania State study, subjects were asked to rate their level of relaxation after listening to fifteen minutes of one of five types of music. The researchers observed that "No single type of music was found to lead to significantly more relaxation. . . . *The most important factor in relaxation was the degree of liking for the music.*"[17]

Their conclusion? "Individual preferences must be considered when using music to aid relaxation." Music that has been categorized by some people as soothing music may not be soothing to everyone.[18]

More recent research has yielded the same conclusion. A 1988 study by Dr. Suzanne B. Hanser[19] reviewed over eighty published articles and books on stress reduction through music. She concluded that no single style of music would reduce anxiety in everyone. Different people respond to music in different ways. She summarized her findings as follows: "The controversy surrounding the effectiveness of music in reducing stress becomes a question of selecting the most appropriate auditory stimulus for a given person in a particular setting."[20]

According to Hanser, the claim that New Age composers' long themes and slow tempos best soothe and relax the listener is not supported by the evidence. Similarly, classical music may soothe some and irritate others. We would assume that rock would produce varied reactions as well. Individual taste must be taken into account when discussing the psychological effects of music. A style that bothers me could very well soothe someone else after a trying day at work.

MUSIC AND MOOD CHANGES

Some people claim that classical music produces good moods and that rock music produces bad moods. Yet psychological studies indicate that a single style of music can generate diverse moods in listeners. Indeed, what we today call "classical music" involves many different musical styles.

A study at the University of São Paulo in 1985 found that a piece by Brahms produced sleepiness and "diminished feelings of obligation and surprise" in a group of eighty people between the ages of forty-eight to eighty-three. A Tchaikovsky piece "produced more activated states (for example, interest, desire, sexual attraction, anger, fright)" in the same group of subjects.[21] Here we have two different styles of music, both called classical, generating very different responses.

A 1952 study found that classical and American folk music produced moods ranging from stimulated to reverent, from nostalgic to irritated, from eerie to upbeat, from depressed to happy.[22] Nowhere have I found evidence that one style causes a universal mood response.

It would seem that similar results could be obtained with exposure to a wide range of rock songs. For those who appreciate the genre, some songs would produce nostalgia and others excitement. But these emotions are not in themselves right or wrong. In fact, excitement about what is good is encouraged in the Bible. The worship of the ancient Hebrews was often characterized by healthy exuberance. They danced, clapped, blew trumpets loudly, and clashed cymbals as they rejoiced before the Lord (Ps. 98:4; 149:3; 150; 1 Chron. 15:16; 2 Chron. 5:12). Let's take care not to equate spirituality with serenity.

Emotions are not wrong in and of themselves. Ethics come in when the performer or composer decides what subject matter to link with the emotion that is being generated.

CAUTIONS ON CITING PSYCHOLOGICAL STUDIES

Having scrutinized Dr. Diamond's conclusions, we can identify with the reviewer in *Publisher's Weekly* who referred to Diamond's behavioral kinesiology as "a bizarre therapeutic system."[23] According to John Ankerberg and John Weldon, "No basic teaching or practice of applied kinesiology"— of which Diamond's behavioral kinesiology is an extension—"can be scientifically established as true, and scientific testing of A.K. claims proves that they are false."[24]

With all of this in mind, it is regrettable that trusted Christian leaders have uncritically accepted and taught Diamond's theories as established fact. We should learn an important lesson from this study: All too often we embrace psychological studies as if they are indisputable proof of some theory. However, in the field of psychology, later findings sometimes modify or even reverse the conclusions of earlier studies as more variables are controlled and new factors are considered.

For instance, prior to the North Carolina State experiment cited earlier, a similar study concluded that rock music hindered vigilant performance. However, in this earlier study the researchers failed to account for an important variable that significantly affected the results: familiarity. The early researchers concluded that the subject's performance was affected by the style. Actually, later research determined that familiar music was affecting the subjects differently from unfamiliar music, regardless of the style.

This refining process is typical of psychological studies. Researchers state their conclusions tentatively, knowing that later experiments will certainly refine, and possibly discount, their studies.[25] Those of us who are nonspecialists would do well to resist the temptation to quote an isolated study to substantiate a controversial position.[26]

APPLICATIONS FOR THE CHURCH

In sum, my research fails to yield solid evidence, based on psychological studies, that one style of music is in itself healthier than another style. Studies sensationalized by critics have been weighed on the scales and found wanting.[27]

However, in examining this literature we have uncovered two further insights that shed light on the present controversy. First, if people's response

to music is highly individual and based upon their
preference and familiarity, then we can better understand people's varied reactions to new musical
forms. Those who are unaccustomed to popular
music or who prefer other kinds of music may well
be irritated and frustrated by it. Even so, it would
be wrong for them to conclude that everyone is
affected the same way. The psychological evidence
simply does not support the idea that any one style
produces a universal response.

Second, church leaders may be able to communicate more effectively with certain age and cultural
groups by using musical styles that appeal to those
particular groups. Some groups may well find that
traditional church music hinders their worship if
the style does not appeal to those who are listening.
We must be sensitive to the tastes of the people we
are targeting if we want our music ministries to be
effective.

3

CHARGES OF MORAL CORRUPTION

A Christian is a perfectly free lord of all, subject to none. A Christian is a perfectly dutiful servant of all, subject to all.

Martin Luther

But whoever causes one of these little ones who believe in Me to stumble, it is better for him that a heavy millstone be hung around his neck, and that he be drowned in the depth of the sea.

Matthew 18:6

SENSUALITY

THE CRITIC: "OK, perhaps our case from psychology was overrated. But obviously secular rock concerts breed every sort of atrocity. The sensuous beat evidently arouses passions that would otherwise lie dormant, making it unwise to use such styles for Christian purposes."

Some critics claim that the American Medical Association has recently linked the rock beat with drug abuse and immorality. They cite a newspaper report of an article published in the *Journal of the*

American Medical Association as proof.[1] But the primary document was careful to make no direct causal relationship between a style of music and deleterious behavior.

Rather, the report warned of the potential impact of secular rock bands that present inaccurate and unhealthy views of the world. Concern was expressed for youth who have immersed themselves "into a heavy metal subculture with such bands as Slayer and Metallica." The writers concluded: "Evidence, though anecdotal, suggests that these adolescents may be at risk for drug abuse or even participation in satanic activities."[2]

Hear! Hear! I concur wholeheartedly with this article and will reiterate this warning in chapter 12 in exposing the evils perpetrated by many popular musicians.

However, this article says nothing of beats or styles that are harmful in and of themselves. Christian rock was not even considered. To take a study of the negative reactions to the likes of Slayer and Metallica and conclude that Petra is harmful is on a par with taking a study of the negative impact of X-rated movies and concluding that *Bambi* is harmful.

On the contrary, the only study I am aware of that has compared teens who listen to contemporary Christian music with those who prefer secular music found that those listening to the Christian music tended to have higher grade point averages.[3]

EXPECTATIONS, INCITEMENTS, AND ATMOSPHERES

I have found no studies linking sensuality with a particular musical style or beat in itself. Apparently, the wild atmosphere generated at some secular rock concerts leads some critics to assume that the culprit is the style of music. But is it possible that the ungodly response is caused primarily by a combination of the sensuous lyrics, the expectations of those in attendance, and the life-styles of the performers?

People go to a Rolling Stones concert for the wild atmosphere as much as for the music. When they arrive, they are ready to party! As they enter the auditorium, they find thousands of others who have come with the same expectations, and the performers encourage the atmosphere by their words and actions. Prince seduces the audience with his hedonistic philosophy and sexually explicit antics on stage. Cher dresses to kill. The Doors encouraged rebellion.

We propose that the music style itself does not elicit the ungodly response at a rock concert any more than country music makes people drink and dance in a country night club. It is the intentions of the people and the incitements of the performers that govern the response rather than the style of music.

Many anthropological studies support this proposal. Whereas the people of one culture may react with strong emotion or even lose consciousness

CONTEMPORARY CHRISTIAN MUSIC UNDER FIRE

when exposed to a certain musical style in a particular setting, people of another culture may not be affected at all.[4]

This hypothesis can be supported by comparing the response to the Beatles' music during their performing days with the response to their music today. Critics have pointed to the chaotic reaction to the Beatles as evidence that rock stirs people up in their sensual nature. Yet if you watch people calmly listen to the Beatles today, you will wonder what all the fuss was about. If the problem was inherently in the style, there should be no difference in the response people have to the music today from the response they had in the sixties. Once again we see that the problem was not with the kind of music, but with the attitudes and expectations of the people coupled with the performance of the band.

Granted, much of rock music does generate an exciting atmosphere, but excitement is not wrong in itself. We have observed that a healthy exuberance often accompanies Old Testament worship. Excitement itself is neutral, but a rock artist has the opportunity to channel that excitement toward positive or negative ends.

The spoken word is powerful—"Death and life are in the power of the tongue," according to Proverbs 18:21—and Hitler channeled the excitement generated by his charismatic speeches to further his malevolent cause. The medium (a motivating

26

speech) was not the culprit. Rather, the message sent through the medium was to blame.

Most people who attend a Carmen concert will find it impossible to remain seated. The atmosphere is electric, but the emotions are directed toward the things we ought to be excited about: standing for Jesus, warring against the principalities and powers of evil, and celebrating our final victory to come.

SYNCOPATION, THE BEAT, AND SENSUALITY

A syncopated beat is often isolated as the root of the problem. But syncopation is actually found in many styles of music, including classical ("The Hallelujah Chorus") and accepted hymnody ("When Jesus Came into My Heart"). Are critics willing to jettison all music containing syncopation? We have found no studies linking syncopation with negative reactions.

Further, "the beat" of rock music is often identical to the beat of softer music played in doctors' offices or department stores. For the most part, drums have become accepted by our society as a whole. Thus, many who denounce the beat of rock music probably accept a softer form of the same beat in their easy-listening music. In fact, many church musicals also include this beat. It is inconsistent to accept the beat of one style and denounce the beat of the other when the beat is essentially the same.

It is interesting to observe that soft music is more conducive to sensuality than hard music. Motion picture directors are experts at connecting the appropriate music with a scene. Soft music generally accompanies love scenes to make the audience feel a oneness with the movie.

In Part 3 we will find that the association of popular styles with worldly practices has often led Christian leaders to wrongly assume a cause-effect relation between the two. At one point in church history, certain musical intervals were thought to be sensual.[5] The Babylonian Talmud refers to a woman's voice as "a sexual incitement." The early church forbade the men and women to sing together, because it was seen as a symbol of sexual union.[6] Carlstadt stated, "Relegate organs, trumpets, and flutes to the theater. Better one heartfelt prayer than a thousand cantatas of the Psalms. The lascivious notes of the organ awaken thoughts of the world."[7]

But what seemed intuitively obvious to Carlstadt—the sensual nature of organ music—was actually a misguided assumption. Others condemned Luther's lute, the violin ("the devil's fiddle"), and other instruments for the same reason. Let us take care not to perpetuate the same error in our own time.

DEMONIC INFLUENCES

THE CRITIC: "But what about the missionary's children who brought some contemporary Christian music back to the mission field? When the tribespeople heard it, they questioned why the children were calling demons."

Al Menconi, author, seminar leader, and special-

ist in contemporary music, traced down the offensive album and discovered that, far from what most
people would identify as rock today, the guilty
album was an early seventies production including
such songs as "When the Roll Is Called Up Yonder"
and "He's Everything to Me." The record features
such performers as Cliff Barrows, the Spurlows,
and Ralph Carmichael. Menconi observed that "if
this song"—speaking of "He's Everything to Me"—
"is demonic, nearly every Christian choir in America must be in danger."[8]

But other witnesses have come forward to testify
in behalf of the demonic beat theory, and a more
careful response is in order. Stephen Maphosah
grew up in Zimbabwe, Africa, playing the drums to
call up evil spirits in village worship rituals. After
converting to Christianity, he sampled ten of the
most popular contemporary Christian albums and
classified them all as "unacceptable and offensive."[9]

By way of response let's first assume the validity
of the testimony. This man grew up in a tribe that
used a specific beat to summon demons. Does this
prove that the beat is inherently demonic, summon-
ing evil spirits regardless of context or culture? One
way to support this hypothesis would be to show
that this same beat is used in many isolated cultures
for demonic worship. If the same beat arose inde-
pendently in a variety of cultures, then credence
would be lent to the theory. In order to draw this
conclusion, we need the perspective of a person
familiar with the music of many cultures to deter-

mine if the "demonic beat" is consistent from tribe to tribe.

G. William Supplee, adjunct professor of music at Columbia Bible College and Seminary, grew up in India and has since taught and studied music in over fifty different cultures. In researching the demon-beat theory, he first isolated the beat used for demon worship in one tribe. He found that in addition to the beats that were used to summon demons, certain tunes and even colors were also associated with the practice. But as he compared these associations with those of other tribes, he found that, for example, just down the ridge, another tribe associated the same tune with play that the former tribe had used for demonic worship.

The bottom line? After examining many cultures, painstakingly recording and comparing their drum patterns, Supplee could find no consistent beat from culture to culture for calling up demons. In fact, the call for demons was associated with rites other than drum beats in some tribes. A series of notes may have functioned for the practice in one culture. There was simply no consistent "demon beat."[10]

Guilbert Rouget, chairman of the Department of Ethnomusicology at the Musée de l'Homme in Paris, thoroughly analyzed the relationship between possession and music. His work should be read by every adherent to the demon beat theory. In his book, *Music and Trance*, Rouget carefully documents the great diversity of music associated with trance and spirit possession worldwide and offers several pertinent insights.

First, Rouget agrees with Supplee that there is no consistent demon beat.[11] Beats associated with possession ceremonies vary widely from culture to culture. Second, many cultures associate instruments other than drums with possession. One uses a sacred bell, another a fiddle; one a loud gourd rattle, another a gentle chanting accompanied by a faint zither; one a flute, another an oboe; one a lute, another a rattle. Some possessions are accompanied by singing with no instruments.[12] Rouget concludes: "There are as many different kinds of possession music as there are different possession cults."[13]

Apparently Maphosah used a beat for his pagan worship that was similar to the beats found in some rock songs. Having grown up with this association, there was obvious confusion when he found the same beat used in some Christian songs. Similarly, if a member of the VaNdau tribe of Mozambique were to hear a flute used in a Christian context, he may very well object, "Why are you appeasing the spirits?" since the flute serves this purpose in his tribe.[14] If Maphosah reacts negatively to a beat merely because his tribe uses it with demonic rites, then it cannot be assumed that the beat itself has inherent qualities that appeal to demons.

STUMBLING BLOCKS
On the surface, the issue of stumbling blocks would

seem to make the music debate an open-and-shut case.

Premise 1: The Bible states it is wrong to offend fellow believers.

Premise 2: Believers testify that contemporary Christian music has offended them.

Therefore: It is wrong to use contemporary Christian music.

To properly evaluate this view, we must take a closer look at the Scriptures dealing with the relations between "weaker brothers," those who wrongly believe that a morally neutral practice is sinful, and "stronger brothers," those who understand that a certain practice is morally neutral and can be participated in with a clear conscience (see Rom. 14:1–15:7 and 1 Cor. 8–10.) For the sake of argument, we will assume that contemporary Christian music is not wrong in itself, but that it has been a stumbling block to some who believe it to be wrong.

The weaker brother of Romans 14 wrongly held that eating meat was wrong, but the fact that his belief was wrong didn't give the stronger brother the right to regard the weaker with contempt (vv. 3, 10) or to hurt his brother (vv. 13, 15). Rather, the stronger brother is exhorted to be careful not to let what is good for him become a spiritual hindrance to the weak. Thus, although a person may have the freedom under God to listen to contemporary Christian music, there may be situations in which he must give up his right. The deciding factor is the potential harm to a weaker brother who may be hurt or led to listen to music that is sinful for him.

This leads to a question: Is the stronger brother called, then, to give up every practice that can be shown by testimony to be offensive to other believers? A closer look at the biblical data reveals some limitations that must be taken into account.[15]

1. *Geographic or social distance limits responsibility.* Paul advised the Corinthian congregation to "eat anything that is sold in the meat market" (1 Cor. 10:25). Yet, Paul knew that some in Rome were vegetarian by conviction (Rom. 14:2). Apparently the scruples of some should concern only those with whom they come in contact, not all believers everywhere.

Believers in Cuba do not play dominoes. The Amish do not wear neckties. Many staunchly contend that the King James Version is the only true English Bible. But since to my knowledge none of these groups are affected by my noncompliance, in my local situation I have no responsibility to limit my freedom in those areas. Similarly, if contemporary Christian music is used to target those who have no problems with it, then no stumbling block has been laid.

2. *A mere difference of taste should not limit freedom.* Some who denounce Christian rock are not truly hurt by advocates of contemporary styles. Neither are they tempted to begin listening to the "offensive" music. This group simply never enjoyed it in the first place.

No church can acquiesce to the personal preferences of every member. Some like a more formal, liturgical service. Some want more praise choruses, others, more traditional hymns or "good ol' gospel music."

Although preferences need to be considered when planning a service, we must recognize that this is not a weaker brother/stronger brother issue in the biblical sense. The true weaker brother believes that the practice is sinful, not just inappropriate.

3. *Sometimes accommodation is not the best approach for building up an overscrupulous individual.* Although in general we are to "give no offense either to Jews or to Greeks or to the church of God" (1 Cor. 10:32), the underlying principle is to seek "the profit of the many, that they may be saved" (1 Cor. 10:33). Sometimes our accommodation is not the best way to profit a person.

Jesus knowingly offended (Greek word for "stumbling" in other contexts) the Pharisees by declaring all foods clean (Matt. 15:12). Apparently in this case the need to correct false theology took precedence over the potential offense. Had Jesus complied with the dietary scruples of the Pharisees, he might well have reinforced a tradition that falsely emphasized external cleanness over internal holiness (see Matt. 15:17-18).

Jesus shocked the spiritual elite of his day with his proximity to sinners, his dealings with Samaritans, and his "violations" of the Sabbath. Sometimes our accommodations can distort the truth for onlookers. In such cases, weaker brothers need to grow up, and it's our responsibility to educate and challenge them in a spirit of love rather than accommodate their sometimes immature whims.

The guiding principles that we should follow are that we are to edify believers and win the lost. Many of today's worshipers testify to the positive impact of contemporary Christian music in their lives. Al Menconi has received over thirty-five hundred testimonies to this fact at the time of this writing.[16]

If 95 percent of a congregation testifies that praise choruses and contemporary specials are the best music tools for drawing their hearts toward God in worship, why should this format be dropped due to the complaints of a disgruntled few? What if changing the format to appease the 5 percent hindered the 95 percent in their worship? Surely this is not wise.

In this situation, perhaps the church leadership should help educate the small group as to the legitimacy of such forms of music. Should the group retain their convictions, they need to learn the scriptural responsibilities of weaker brothers toward the stronger—do not condemn (Rom. 14:3), do not instigate division (14:19), etc.—in order to preserve unity in the body.

4. *Contradictory scruples can make accommodation impossible in some cases.* Many Baptists are convinced that an evangelistic invitation should be

offered at the close of every service. Many Calvin-
ists (some of whom are Baptist) hold just as
strongly that no invitations should be given.
Regarding musical style, some believe that the best
church music is traditional hymns; others believe
just as strongly that the church must appeal to each
individual culture. Some argue that instruments
detract from worship; others contend we have a
biblical mandate to use instruments. Obviously we
cannot appease all parties in one service. Either we
use instruments or we don't, and if both groups are
in the same congregation, one group may be hurt.

5. *The sheer number of scruples can make total
compliance a distortion of the nature of the Christian life.* Some believers hold strong convictions
against wearing blue jeans (they are a sign of rebellion), men wearing hair over the ears or having
beards, women wearing pants or wearing makeup,
using any instruments in the church (including
pianos and organs), reading new translations of the
Bible (meaning any translation done after 1611), or
singing hymns (the Psalms alone should be sung).
Whenever a congregation grows beyond an aggregate total of one, there will be multiple heartfelt
opinions on a variety of issues.

If we become preoccupied with rules and prohibitions, the nature of the Christian life ceases to be
what God purposed it to be. It was for freedom
that Christ set us free, not to be returned to bondage (Gal. 5:1).

Many Christians, due to bad associations in their

lives before they were Christians, are troubled by practices in which others feel free to participate. Personal associations can place "stumbling block potential" on many items that are in themselves neutral. One counselor relates how even a rope can trigger evil thoughts in the mind of a sadomasochist.[17] For such an individual, we must consider his problem in our dealings with him. But should his problem deprive all youth groups from enjoying a tug-of-war at a summer camp? If the association were widespread, maybe. But the extent of the problem must be found before we restrict all use of ropes in churches. Many people nationwide may testify to this problem, but few or none may be affected on the local level.

One person associated classical music with the evil of his pre-Christian days and so felt obligated to abstain from certain classical pieces. Similarly, some have given up playing sports such as football for recreation. Their high school training in the sport was so "win oriented" that to this day they can't participate without rekindling the "killer instinct."

But such associations are so individualized and varied that it would be virtually impossible to live a life-style void of all these practices. Out of love for the brother who associated classical music with the world, I would gladly refrain from such when he was in my car or home. But I would feel no obligation to burn my classical tapes and never listen to them again.

Similarly, some have associated the rock style with the non-Christian life-style. While we should please our brother in a personal situation, his weakness should not keep us from listening in every situation.

6. *Finally, the biblical precedent of winning the lost may lead us to use methods or adopt life-styles that certain believers might question.* How do we decide when to exercise our freedom and when to restrict ourselves in a controversial area? For Paul, the decision hinged, in part, on his effectiveness in reaching the lost (1 Cor. 9). He became like a Jew in order to reach Jews more effectively; he became like those without the law in order to reach those without the law (1 Cor. 9:20-21). Many in the first century used the detailed, pharisaical laws to condemn others and promote salvation by works; others used their freedom from the law as an opportunity for unbridled sin. Paul knew that the keeping or ignoring of these laws was neither wrong nor right in itself; but imagine the problems others may have had with this practice.

If a Gentile were to see Paul diligently keeping all of the Jewish laws, the Gentile could have easily associated his practices with the legalism that was so prevalent at that time. On the other hand, the Jew might find Paul relating to the lawless Gentile and stumble over his disregard for laws important to the Jew. The Jew might be tempted to disregard laws that to him were still important, and his conscience would be defiled. Still, Paul knew he had to take the risk to reach the Gentile who might have otherwise interpreted Paul's law keeping as legalism.

So today there are those unbelievers who stumble over the church's traditional music, which they consider antiquated. There are also vibrant Christians who claim they are hindered in their worship by traditional worship styles. They may have found salvation through a ministry that happened to use contemporary music, and now they falsely associate traditional music with deadness and hypocrisy and find such worship forms detrimental to their spiritual life.

This is not a hypothetical situation. Testimonies along this line can be documented.[18] So by removing a hindrance from before those who disapprove of contemporary Christian music, we may in fact place a hindrance before those who disapprove of traditional music.

Jesus ate with sinners, knowing full well that many religious people would be offended, but there was a more important issue at stake than pleasing the overscrupulous Pharisees. He was concerned with finding the lost coin, leaving the ninety-nine to find the one lost sheep.

We can't paralyze ministries that are reaching thousands through their music because of isolated individuals who blame their fall on the style of music. To do so would be to risk laying a stumbling block before multitudes of individuals who may not respond to any other style of ministry.

Some churches in the late sixties and early seventies actually required men to cut their hair above their ears to join their church. At least one church went so far as to have a barber chair installed to ensure conformity. One can but wonder how many stumbled over the barber chair as they considered the message of grace.

Famous English preacher Charles H. Spurgeon was castigated for using London's Surrey Gardens Music Hall for his services, but, once again, there was a more important issue at stake: the churches couldn't contain the crowds who came to listen to his message. He chose to remain despite the opposition.

Some people were offended by the use of secular tunes and instruments by William Booth, the founder of the Salvation Army. But a more important issue was at stake here as well: reaching the unreached masses who weren't responding to traditional forms of evangelism. The number of conversions through Booth's ministry was impressive, but the priority of evangelism had to be established as they selected their methodology.

Today innovative churches are reaching multitudes through contemporary concerts and worship services that target unreached segments of our society.[19] Had there been no concerts, out of deference to scattered critics, one wonders if these unbelievers would ever have been reached.

SUMMARY

We have seen that our response to those who object

to contemporary forms of music is not quite as simple as some have made it. Our guiding purpose should always be to build up the brethren, promote harmony, and win the lost. At times we must sacrifice our own rights in order to reach these ends.

If a traditionally minded church has made it clear to an innovative pastor that popular music styles hinder their ability to worship and hurt them, then the pastor would be wise to either cease using contemporary forms, restrict such forms to target ministries, or move to another ministry that is open to such forms.

Sometimes evangelistic contexts must determine the appropriate music. At other times, an over-scrupulous brother must be educated for the benefit of the entire body.

Is Christian rock a stumbling block? It can be. But so can organs, ties, classical music, or dominoes. Only a prayerful application of the whole counsel of the Word of God to each situation can ensure that we are in the center of God's perfect will.

4

CHARGES OF WORLDLINESS

*Do not love the world, nor the things in the world.
If anyone loves the world, the love of the Father is
not in him.*

1 John 2:15

THE CRITIC: "Christian rock artists admit to imitating the world's styles and using them for godly ends. But adopting the world's methods and using them for God is blatant compromise. The biblical mandate in Romans 12:2 is clear: 'Do not be conformed to this world.'"

On the surface, this attack appears insurmountable: "You can have your contemporary music or the Bible, but not both." But upon closer inspection, some serious flaws in this mentality emerge.

PROBLEMS WITH A POPULAR DEFINITION
It would be incorrect to interpret *the world,* as it is used in such passages as Romans 12:1-2 and 1 John 2:15-17, to mean everything that finds its origin or use in the sinful world. Consider the fact that both of these passages were penned in Greek,

43

a language developed by pagans and spoken by pagans. Roman officials used this language to plan military offenses and subjugate innocent nations. Materialistic merchants made their silver-tongued pitches in Greek as they ripped off naive consumers. Pagan deities were worshiped, prostitutes were paid for their services, and the gospel was preached all in the Greek tongue. If we were to adhere to the above interpretation of *the world,* then the use of Greek for anything of God would be wrong.

Even today, Bible translators translate the Scriptures into many languages. The exact grammatical structures that once were used to worship pagan deities and tell dirty jokes are being used to convey the Word of God.

Even beyond using the Greek language, Paul quoted pagan poets and philosophers such as Epicurus and the Stoics (see Acts 17:16-34). Apparently the apostle did not consider everything developed or used by evil men as worldly. At least language was viewed as a neutral medium.

But what of *practices* developed by the world? G. R. Beasley Murray's monumental work, *Baptism in the New Testament,* traces the antecedents of Christian baptism to ancient pagan religions.[1] Although the symbolism attached to the early use of this rite might be considered blasphemous to the Christian, later the Hebrews adopted this practice and, by New Testament times, John the Baptist and Jesus had no qualms about taking this rite of pagan origins and redeeming it for a beautiful picture of Christian conversion.

So, separation from the world cannot mean distancing ourselves from everything that finds its origin or use in the sinful world. Otherwise, Paul, John the Baptist, and even Jesus, would be guilty of worldliness.

DEFINING "THE WORLD"

So what is this *world* from which Christians are to separate themselves? The Greek word for world, *kosmos,* carries different meanings in different contexts. In John 3:16 we read that God loved the world; in 1 John 2:15 the Christian is warned not to love the world. The same Greek word is used, but with different meanings.

We find the same phenomenon in English when we say we *run* in a race (a leg race), *run* to the store (driving), *run* out of gas (depleting the supply), and get a *run* in a pair of hose (tear). When a word can carry multiple meanings, the context must determine the definition.

So what does Paul mean by his reference to the world in Romans 12? Regarding this passage, commentator Robert Haldane writes, "This prohibition, however, respects those things only that are sinful, and does not require singularity in the Christian in anything that is not contrary to the law of Christ."[2] Paul is not urging the Christian to exhibit nonconformity in all clothing fashions or recreation, but only in those fashions or types of recreation that are sinful.

Well then, what of John's use of *the world* in 1 John 2? F. F. Bruce describes it thus: "Worldliness, it must be emphasized in the face of much superficial thought and language on the subject, does not lie in things we do or in places we frequent; it lies in the human heart, in the seat of human affections and attitudes." For example, regarding material gain, "Worldliness does not reside in 'things,' but it does certainly reside in our concentration on things."[3]

I. Howard Marshall defines it a little more broadly as "'disobedience to God's rule of life,' and its presence is to be discerned by asking, 'What is God's will?' and not by making a human list of taboos."[4]

In other words, worldliness involves participating in those attitudes or those activities of the world that God has labeled "sin," either by direct teaching or by principle. Those who assume a broader definition (such as "all that is produced by or used by evil people") cannot live consistently with their proposal.

LET'S BE CONSISTENT

Josh McDowell has toured with the Christian rock band Petra. When doing so, he often invites local ministers to a meeting prior to the concert to

answer questions concerning their ministry. When
critics complain that Christian bands often look
like secular bands, Josh is apt to catch a pastor in
an inconsistency.

> *He scans the room and finds a gentleman in*
> *typical reverend rig—gray pinstripe suit,*
> *Oxford shirt, power tie, wing tips. "Sir, are*
> *you a pastor?" A nod in the affirmative. "You*
> *know, I can't begin to tell you apart from the*
> *world. In America, every single pastor who*
> *gets up on Sunday morning looks like the*
> *world—IBM from the word go. And when I*
> *visit your churches, I have to dress like I'm*
> *heading for Wall Street or most of you*
> *wouldn't let me speak to your congregation."[5]*

Those who advocate nonconformity to the world
should apply that mandate across the board in their
lives. However, even those who have "separated"
themselves from the world's style of music enjoy traditional hymns on the world's tape players, run by
electricity from the world's generators, powered by
the same brand of amplifiers that help generate the
songs of the Rolling Stones. In other words, many
things that have been developed and used by the
world are morally neutral in themselves. A scalpel
is an instrument of healing in the hands of the sur-
geon, but it is an instrument of terror in the hands
of the Nazi war criminal.

WHAT IS COMPROMISE?

One of the strongest reasons for advocating non-conformity is the concern about compromise. Christians want to avoid compromising, thus weakening, their faith and witness. Take the example of the movie theater. Picture Bob as he goes to see a sensual R-rated movie on Thursday night. He buys a ticket, enters the theater, buys popcorn and a Coke, steps on a wad of chewing gum, spills a little Coke onto the already sticky floor, and sits down to fill his mind with all that is contrary to Philippians 4:8.

Friday rolls around and Bob decides to attend another movie. He enters the same theater, buys popcorn and Coke, steps on a wad of chewing gum, spills a little Coke onto the already sticky floor, and sits down to view *The Prodigal,* a Billy Graham film, which presents a clear evangelistic message and leads to a change in Bob's eternal destiny. Note that all of the aspects of movie theaters are present in both cases. The only difference is the *content* of the movie.

Is Billy Graham compromising by using movies, a medium that seems to promote evil even more frequently than contemporary music? No. A movie can be used to convey either good or evil. What then constitutes compromise? Suppose a Christian organization were to produce a movie that promoted sexual sin—or some other activity contrary to God's laws—and ended with a gospel presentation? This would be using what is worldly (a script that defies the teaching of Phil. 4:8) to promote what is good. This is compromise.

A COMMON ERROR

In part three we will learn an important lesson from history: Even godly men have often been blinded to the potential of an instrument or style for good because their generation has misused that instrument or style. If we would only look beyond our own experiences, we might find that if the abuses were eliminated, the instrument or style could become a great tool of God. The lute was transformed into an instrument of refreshment for Luther, the organ into an instrument of praise for Bach, and popular styles into an incredible avenue of evangelism for D.L. Moody and Ira Sankey. Yet, these instruments and styles were banned by many of their contemporaries because of worldly associations.

Using what is neutral in a society as a vehicle for the gospel is not only acceptable; it is sound missionary strategy. Paul did this, as we discussed in chapter 3, when he became "all things to all men" that he might "by all means save some" (1 Cor. 9:22). Paul was willing to subjugate his own lifestyle preference to the greater cause of reaching the lost for Christ.

In the same way today, such powerful media as radio, movies, and contemporary music hold the attention of the world we were sent to reach. Are we willing to follow in Paul's footsteps and "become all things to all men" in order to reach our generation? If so, we must take great care to avoid labeling practices as "worldly" or wrong when they actually are neutral tools, waiting to be used for spreading the gospel.

5

CHARGES OF POOR AESTHETIC QUALITY AND A CAUTIONING INNER WITNESS

I never once flew over the right target without being fired at.

Colonel Nimrod McNair

AESTHETIC QUALITY: IS IT THERE? DO WE NEED IT?

THE CRITIC: "The highest form of music we have today is exemplified in the classics. As Christians, we should strive for musical excellence, and this will never be achieved by stooping to the mediocre artistic level enjoyed by the masses."

Many feel that, in using contemporary music, we are relegating the church to the mediocre or—even worse—to music that is substandard. How do we define "good" music, that is, music that is aesthetically good? Two characteristics of aesthetically good music, which critics have used to degrade contemporary musical styles, are that the music contains rich harmonies, direction, and movement. Let's evaluate these specific characteristics of "good" music.

Rich Harmonies. One opponent of Christian pop music charges that good music should have rich harmonies. Does this mean that music performed with simple harmonies is bad? Was "Edelweiss" in *The Sound of Music* poor music as long as Christopher Plummer sang it to the accompaniment of simple chords on a guitar? On the contrary, the simplicity of the song served its function well—to express the nationalistic sentiment of the Austrian people who were being overtaken by the Nazi regime. It would be unfair to deprive the song of its context and judge it for worth against Beethoven's *Fifth Symphony.* A style should be judged only within the context of its intended function by the people for whom it was designed.[1]

The musician who has made the study and appreciation of "fine" music the focus of his life has not been sidetracked by a worthless endeavor. Even so, he must take care lest his appreciation of the classics lead him to scorn simpler styles. If the highest art forms are always the best church forms, then the *koinē* (common) Greek of the New Testament would have to be deemed substandard when compared to the classical Greek favored by the artsy crowd. Similarly, all the music used to accompany the Psalms during Old Testament times would fall short of this standard of harmonies.[2]

In my opinion, the aerospace engineer who can no longer enjoy flying a kite with his child has lost something. And so has the serious musician who can no longer enjoy "Edelweiss" played as a simple folk song on a classical guitar, accompanied by a voice deemed unacceptable for the opera. The master communicator, capable of producing an oration that will be recorded and preserved for future generations, has lost something if he can no longer be edified by the sincere country preacher who may never have the opportunity to complete a college education. The simple preacher's most excellent efforts would never satisfy the critiques of the serious orators of his day. But then again, his congregation may not respond to the style of the "great" orations. Function must be considered when judging the worth of a style.

Direction and Movement. Other critics of contemporary music argue that "good" music has a definite beginning, builds to a climax, and has a definite conclusion. They claim that fading in reflects evolutionary philosophy, and that fading out symbolizes no final judgment. However, couldn't we just as easily propose that music with a definite beginning symbolizes that God had a beginning, and music with a definite conclusion contradicts the doctrine of eternal punishment and eternal life?

Where do these contentions find their base? Are they imagined to be intuitively obvious to any honest seeker? Or, more likely, since the critic has been trained in Western classical music, does he simply prefer the style of this "good" music, and assume that anyone with good musical taste will concur?

Some cross-cultural observations would support the latter idea.

The Auca Indians have woven intricate drum patterns into their music, beats that we could not fully appreciate nor even perhaps have the skill to duplicate. Thus, if a member of this tribe were to set the standards for "good" music, he would almost certainly deem the paucity of interesting percussion in Western music as rather primitive.

To us, the dominance of drums may detract from what we consider the main course: the melody. To the Auca, the intricate drum patterns may very well *be* the main course. "But the melody line should be dominant!" cries the Westerner. Why? Has psychology demonstrated this to be healthier? No. Does the Bible speak of dominant melodies? No.

"But melody is as central to good music as rhyme is to good poetry," retorts the critic. But rhyme is *not* universally recognized as essential to good poetry. We like rhyme because we have been taught to like rhyme. Are Western standards of beautiful poetry the highest standards? If so, how then would we judge the poetry of the Psalms, where the Hebrew meter differs significantly from our standard patterns and rhyme is not even considered?[3] It is only with great difficulty that we could find beauty in ancient Hebrew poetry. But then again, the ancient Hebrews would have trouble finding any "good" poetry in our forms.

To us, the use of a double negative ("He hasn't got no manners") is obviously an infraction of "good" speech. Not so for the ancient Greeks, who piled up negatives for emphasis. Take a look at John 15:5 in Greek. A literal translation could read, "Apart from Me you cannot do nothing."

Haven't we fallen into ethnocentrism when we take the standards of Western classics and set them up as a universal measuring stick for music, or anything, for that matter? Truly good music must be judged within a form by those who appreciate the form, not by those from without who neither understand nor enjoy the style.[4]

Lessons from History. Before advocates of what is commonly considered "serious" music categorically relegate all new styles to an aesthetic wasteland, they would do well to listen to the critics who pronounced a similar judgment on the innovations of their time.

> *You hear a medley of sounds, a variety of parts, a rumble of harmonies that are intolerable to the ear. One sings in quick tempo, another in slow; one voice has top notes, another deep notes; and as if this was not enough a third remains midway . . . with all the best will in the world, how can the mind see light in this chaos? (Artusi on Monteverdi, 1608)*

> *Three of the movements of Beethoven's symphony in A are without any settled design, confused, full of harsh combinations. (1823)[5]*

*No form, no design, no rhythm, no symmetry
(D'Ortigue on Wagner, 1861)*

*I heard sounds in uninterrupted sequence,
without finding a trace of design, of form, of a
motive, of an accent (a French writer on
Debussy's Pelleas et Melisande, 1902).*

*Unmeaning bunches of notes . . . clotted non-
sense (F. Corder on Schönberg, Musical Quarterly, 1915)*

*Wild insanities such as intellectualized art dis-
dains to touch; and the spirits of ugliness and
destruction abolish the final intellectual bondage of euphony itself. . . . The period of deepest musical degradation . . . shamelessly
avowed in cretinous babble by Schönberg and
Stravinsky (Rutland Boughton, Musical Times,
1922)*[6]

Apparently, it is easy to allow personal preference to establish boundaries for the beautiful that
were never meant to be set.

CAUTIONING WITNESS
There are people, of course, who say about contemporary Christian music: "My spirit does not bear
witness with the Spirit of God that this music is
right." If people have prayed about an issue of controversy and believe that God has not given them

the freedom to participate, we should respect this decision and not press them into something that may be wrong for them.

But should the inner caution on the part of some concerning contemporary music bind all Christians on this issue?

If the Spirit of God were clearly moving among us on this issue, it would seem that there would be some kind of consensus among those who are led of the Spirit—but no such consensus exists. Some have prayed and feel strongly that God wants us to listen exclusively to classical arrangements of traditional hymns. Others are edified by the middle-of-the-road music of the Gaithers, but feel the style of Keith Green moves us into the questionable area of rock. Still others feel great about Keith Green's music but have their inner caution alarms triggered with the style of Petra. Some of us have prayed and fasted about the issue, but feel absolute freedom from the Spirit with this whole range of music styles.

Critics of contemporary Christian music would claim that those who sense no caution light beyond the style of the critic's preference have hardened their hearts through the years so that their sensitivities to the Spirit have grown callous. But how do we know that the opposite is not true—that the critics themselves have refused to accept the possibility that God could use styles they personally dislike? Over time they have developed the conscience of the "weak in faith" of Romans 14, being convinced in their hearts that certain legitimate practices are actually wrong.[7]

Certainly we all need to pray for wisdom and a sensitivity to the Spirit's leading on this issue, but a number of factors should be considered before deciding this issue based on a feeling that you think is the work of the Spirit.

Throughout church history, people have consistently confused the inner leading of the Spirit with the inner cry of their cultural upbringing. The styles of our beloved hymns were once derided as ungodly and even demon-inspired. Apparently these early critics felt an inner peace that they were doing God's bidding, when actually they were resisting His work.

Even today some are reporting that their earlier condemnation of contemporary Christian music was immature and misdirected. After more mature reflection, Josh McDowell had to return to some bands to ask forgiveness for his criticism.[8] Others have gone through a similar transition and now feel confident that the Spirit is using these new forms. But as Spurgeon once said, "It seems odd that certain men who talk so much of what the Holy Spirit reveals to themselves should think so little of what He has revealed to others."[9]

At points of transition in church music styles we have found opponents to all styles, believers who condemn the new styles as inappropriate or even satanic. Because of their cultural conditioning, they were unable to see the Spirit's new work and so committed the serious error of attributing the work of God to the devil. We must be mindful of this tendency as we consider new forms of music today.

Perhaps rather than hastily condemning the whole enterprise as inspired by Satan, it would be wiser to follow the advice given by Gamaliel when a new sect had emerged out of Judaism:

> *Men of Israel, take care what you propose to do with these men. . . . for if this plan or action should be of men, it will be overthrown; but if it is of God, you will not be able to overthrow them; or else you may even be found fighting against God. (Acts 5:35-39)*

6

CHARGES OF BAD ASSOCIATIONS, QUESTIONABLE MOTIVES, AND DANGEROUS LEANINGS

If you have died with Christ to the elementary principles of the world, why, as if you were living in the world, do you submit yourself to decrees, such as, "Do not handle, do not taste, do not touch!"

Colossians 2:20-21

BAD ASSOCIATIONS

THE CRITIC: "Christians should avoid all appearances of evil according to 1 Thessalonians 5:22. Christian musicians are often indistinguishable from evil secular musicians and thus violate this principle."

Critics believe that the use of contemporary music draws the listener—and the performer—into negative associations with worldly groups and music. This concern often is based on 1 Thessalonians 5:22, as stated above. First it should be noted that the verse in 1 Thessalonians has been commonly misconstrued. The Greek word translated "appearance" in the Authorized Version would cause less confusion if it were translated either "kind"[1] or "visible form." M. R. Vincent comments that the Greek word "never has the sense of semblance,"[2] yet many have erred by taking it to mean exactly that. Jesus' proximity to sinners gave him the appearance of evil in the eyes of many, but this was not a sin.

Let us concede that, as a general rule, we should not adopt appearances that give us the look of evil. The question then becomes, Do Christian musicians appear evil to their audiences?

In some aspects of their appearance, there are similarities to ungodly performers. But this is not reason enough for condemnation for, as we have seen, there are also similarities between preachers and evil barons of Wall Street.

There are many characteristics of Christian performers that make their concerts vastly different from the likes of Prince or Iron Maiden. For example, the Christian musicians I have seen dress according to the accepted style of their music, but without the sensual appeal of performers such as Cher. (If some dress sensually, then we should confront them.) The messages of Christian performers also stand in stark contrast to Prince's incitements to illicit sex or Venom's blasphemy. Also, note the absence of cigarette or marijuana smoke at Christian concerts. Transport any Motley Crue groupie from a secular rock concert to a Petra concert, and he or she would immediately sense the contrast in both the performance and the atmosphere.

For now, you may not be able to fully appreciate

these differences. However, the material in chapters 12 through 14 of this book will help you to better understand them. Please withhold judgment on appearances until these chapters paint a clearer picture of today's secular and Christian musicians.

QUESTIONABLE MOTIVES

THE CRITIC: "Christian artists are simply out for the money and popularity."

This is a common attitude of many who seek to condemn participation in contemporary music. Let us agree at the outset that any Christian leader who is a self-seeking materialist should be personally rebuked (as is clearly stated in Matthew 18:15 and Galatians 6:1). If such a person refuses to repent, he or she is disqualified for spiritual leadership (see 1 Tim. 3:3; 6:9).

However, even if some perform Christian music for the wrong motives, this should not call the entire enterprise into question. This makes no more sense than allowing the mishandling of funds by numerous pastors and evangelists to color our opinion of all serving in the ministry. We must be careful not to judge another's heart when we have no solid evidence of his or her fault (1 Cor. 4:5). Some artists undoubtedly make a good bit of money, but often it goes right back into equipment or ministry.

In any profession, what matters most is not how much we make, but how much we keep that places us in the category of a materialist. Those who make accusations regarding motives have yet to forward proof that contemporary Christian performers generally exhibit these sinful motives and practices.

Actually, few Christian artists seem to be in a very good position to have a problem with riches.[3] Christian music specialist Al Menconi claims that "only a handful make a decent living at all."[4] Most are regional artists who either supplement their income with a second job or eke out a living in a ministry with little hope of long-range financial security.

DANGEROUS LEANINGS

THE CRITIC: "In those areas where there is disagreement among Christians, it is always safer to err on the side of the conservative. People are likely to use too much freedom for license, thus making it easy to fall into sin."

Some verbalize this argument, but for many it is an unstated premise that guides many of their decisions in life. In some situations this guideline should be followed; the further we stay away from sin, so it would seem, the less likely we will be to fall into it. For example, this approach is particularly valuable in setting personal guidelines with regard to sexual purity or in setting rules to ensure campus security (for example, no men in women's dorms). However, there are hazards in applying this principle across the board or in an inappropriate manner.

When we lay down an overabundance of extrabiblical rules or give these rules the status of

God's Word, we are no longer on safe ground. As plausible as this approach may seem at first, upon closer examination we find that, while pretending to lead us to safer pastures, it often lures us to a precipice that places us in grave danger. Here are some of those dangers.

The Danger of Phariseeism. There is nothing wrong with strictly following God's Word; it is through obedience that we show our love for Jesus (John 14:15). However, strictly prescribing extrabiblical precepts can plunge us into the sins of the Pharisees, who received no small rebuke from our Lord: "But in vain do they worship Me, teaching as doctrines the precepts of men" (Mark 7:7).

We are quick to side with Jesus against this sect, but have we ever reflected on how easy it would have been to have assisted in developing the extremes that were their downfall? Let's take the observance of the Sabbath, for instance. God gave us a brief, basic command about the Sabbath: rest from work, thus keeping the day set apart unto God. It is rather easy for us to put ourselves in the place of the Old Testament Jew who considered this command and stood in awe of his holy God.

"In order to assure compliance, we need to set some parameters so that we will know when we have profaned this holy day," the ancient Hebrew probably reasoned. "Certainly God would allow us to walk on the Sabbath, but wouldn't walking too much, say, one mile, pass beyond the bounds of rest and become work? So, to make sure we keep the Sabbath holy, let us limit ourselves to a certain distance."

"And beyond our personal standards, wouldn't we likewise protect the members of our synagogue, particularly our youth, by setting parameters and preaching them as authoritative? After all, if we give no specifics as to Sabbath observance, some might take advantage of it. You know, give them an inch and they will take a mile."

It all seems so reasonable. But is such extrabiblical teaching right, especially when it is given the status of divine truth? Well, consider Jesus' reactions. When he came on the scene, the results of such thinking had solidified into a list of prohibitions that clouded the spirit of the commands (for example, the Sabbath was made for man, not the other way around). And Jesus condemned the Pharisees for this.

The Danger of Causing Seekers to Stumble. Besides adding to God's Word, which makes adherence nearly impossible for the believer, overly strict teaching places a stone of stumbling before the world. Christian artist Dana Key relates the disillusionment he encountered early in his spiritual life when he was criticized for wearing blue jeans to church.[5] In his hurt and confusion, he temporarily abandoned the church. Today, with his faith rooted more securely through the passage of years, Key says that he would be willing to wear a double-knit plaid suit or even a toga in order to fellowship with other believers, but as a tender young Christian, the blue jeans issue loomed large on the horizon. This can happen when contemporary music is dogmatically denounced as sin, especially if it is on a par with the blue jeans issue.

The Danger of Paralyzing Effective Ministry. The Pharisees had effectively cut themselves off from productive ministry by distancing themselves from the lost. They used their extrabiblical standards as a shield against unbelievers. When Jesus' proximity to sinners was questioned by the Pharisees, he responded, "It is not those who are healthy who need a physician, but those who are sick; I did not come to call the righteous, but sinners" (Mark 2:17).

The physician who relates only with the healthy will certainly lessen his potential for contracting an illness, but he will be a poor physician. The effective ministry of the gospel to new generations calls for new methods outside the comfort zone of most Christians. Those clinging to the security of the conventional may miss God's move.

In the year 1024, a group of monks who viewed the innovative with suspicion expelled their brother, Guido Arentino, because his simplified method of music instruction enabled his choirboys to learn new melodies with unprecedented speed. Amazed fellow monks connected some type of occult influence with Arentino's achievement and promptly expelled him from their order. Ministry on the cutting edge will always be considered "too close to the world" for the guardians of tradition.[6]

If Spurgeon, one of the greatest preachers of all time, had erred on the side of the conservative he would have never held services in London's Surrey Gardens Music Hall. *The Saturday Review* echoed the sentiment of nearly all the London papers when it printed the following:

> *This hiring of places of amusement for Sunday preaching is a novelty, and a powerful one. It looks as if religion were at its last shift. It is a confession of weakness, rather than a sign of strength. It is not wrestling with Satan in the strongholds . . . but entering into a cowardly truce and alliance with the world.*[7]

But Spurgeon continued in his use of the facility, and the Word of God reached many more ears than a smaller church facility could have afforded. Because of the tradition of men like Spurgeon, we use facilities such as this today to great advantage and with little or no controversy.

If Luther and other reformers had erred on the side of the conservative, we might still be worshiping in Latin. The stricter crowd saw the everyday vernacular as too vulgar for pure worship.[8] Had the strict side prevailed, our hymn style might well never have made it past the Gregorian chant.

Horatious Bonar was considered by Ira Sankey to be "the prince among hymnists" of his time.[9] Yet

Bonar's church erred on the "safe" side and restricted themselves exclusively to singing Psalms. Bonar's songs have blessed many generations and still grace the pages of hymnbooks to this day, but the blessing bypassed his own congregation. Could it be that a blessing is bypassing many churches today because of a similar error?

It is true that the nearer one draws to God, the more he abhors the sins of the world (Rom. 12:9). Satan, though, is ever so subtle. He realizes the futility of drawing some believers back into the immorality of the world, and so he holds out the promise of greater purity through another form of worldliness: legalism. "If a few rules are a good thing," his persuasive reasoning goes, "then an abundance of rules must be a great thing!"

The end result of this reasoning can be a crippling legalistic mind-set disguised as holiness and purity. The further one follows this path, the more the essence of the Christian life becomes the age-old "Do not handle, do not taste, do not touch!" rather than "righteousness and peace and joy in the Holy Spirit" (Rom. 14:17).

Some may be shocked to find that worldliness in the Scriptures is not limited to excessive license, but also includes a preoccupation with extrabiblical rules. Paul charged the Colossians: "See to it that no one takes you captive through philosophy and empty deception, according to the tradition of men, according to the elementary principles of the world, rather than according to Christ" (Col. 2:8).

"World" here is a translation of *kosmos,* the same Greek word used in 1 John 2:15. But the Colossian context concerns people who have gone overboard with extrabiblical rules: what to eat, what to drink, how to observe the Sabbath, self-abasement, and misguided decrees as seen in Colossians 2:8-23.[10] "These are matters which have, to be sure, the appearance of wisdom in self-made religion and self-abasement and severe treatment of the body, but are of no value against fleshly indulgence" (Col. 2:23).

So we must take care lest our flight from the world land us in the lap of a more subtle but just as deadly form of the world. "Legalism, asceticism, and ritualism are the world's feeble and enfeebling substitutes for true religion," says R. V. G. Tasker, emeritus professor of New Testament exegesis. "Similarly, false prophets who advocate such things . . . will always be listened to by those who belong to this world."[11]

Paul states that "in later times some will fall away from the faith, paying attention to deceitful spirits and doctrines of demons" (1 Tim. 4:1). Just what is it that these individuals with "seared con- sciences" (4:2) will be advocating? A new hedo- nism? Guess again. It is a new legalism that will include such strictures as abstaining from certain foods (4:3).

Apparently things that may seem trivial to us (a few scruples being taught about food restrictions) are considered major heresies ("doctrines of demons) in God's estimation. The adherence to an authoritative teaching of principles that are more strict than the Bible's is far from safe ground according to the Scriptures—rather, it is a subtle form of worldliness instigated by the enemy.

It is *not* safe to err on the side of the conservative. It is never safe to err.

PART TWO

A BIBLICAL PERSPECTIVE

7

The Bible on Music

All Scripture is inspired by God and profitable for teaching, for reproof, for correction, for training in righteousness; that the man of God may be adequate, equipped for every good work.

2 Timothy 3:16-17

For the great part of this book's readership, ultimate authority rests not in the passing whims of psychology or the dogmatic assertions of the musically elite, but in God's revelation to people, the Bible. Whether the issue involves finances, relationships, or music, God's Word is "a lamp to my feet, and a light to my path" (Ps. 119:105).

The need to focus on the biblical data is especially keen in the area of music, since subjective feelings and cultural bias have historically clouded the truth. Calvin limited corporate praise to metrical versions of the Psalms. After all, the Psalter is the Bible's book of praise. How could any human composition compare with the text of the very Word of God? The conclusion sounded reasonable to Calvin and multitudes of believers who followed his teachings, but was it biblical? Did the Bible itself place this restriction on corporate worship?

History helps us realize that one's feelings, however strong, cannot be solely relied upon in this area. Our own upbringing and culture grasp us so firmly that it is difficult to make objective decisions. We desperately need to take our subjectively based opinions and place them under the scrutiny of the objective Word of God. Only then can we separate fact from fantasy, truth from speculation.

In this chapter we will survey what the Bible says about music and praise, searching for revealed truth concerning the importance, forms (styles, instruments, methods), and functions (goals, purposes, uses) of music. While striving for completeness, the wealth of biblical materials guarantees that certain Scriptures will be overlooked, so the following study should be viewed as representative rather than exhaustive.

THE PRIORITY OF PRAISE

Praise through music is not on the periphery of God's plan. Luther was on target when he sought to extol music in the loftiest of terms and called it "a noble gift of God, next to theology."

In the temple worship of the old covenant, 4,000 Levites were appointed to praise God with instruments (1 Chron. 23:5) and 288 trained singers with their voices (1 Chron. 25:7). The very magnitude of this enterprise demonstrates the priority the Father puts on praise.

The longest book in the Bible is the Psalms, the hymnbook of the ancient Hebrews. Would so much space be devoted to a subject that was not near to the heart of God?

The sacrificial system was central to the service of the old covenant, but King David saw worship through song as giving more pleasure to God. In Psalm 69:30-31 the inspired psalmist wrote,

> *I will praise the name of God with song,*
> *And shall magnify Him with thanksgiving.*
> *And it will please the Lord better than an ox*
> *Or a young bull with horns and hoofs.*

The Scriptures do not picture the Father as yawning through the praise portion of our service in anticipation of the spoken Word of God. Rather, the Father is actively seeking true worshipers, who will worship Him in spirit and in truth (see John 4:20-24).

The more we trivialize praise, either through relegating it to a small slot in the service or through shoddy preparation, the further we fall short of the biblical standard. Worship is primary.

FORM IN WORSHIP

But just how should we use music in the church and in daily life? God could have inspired a writer to include in our Scriptures an authoritative order of service, including the songs to be sung, the instruments to be played, and the appropriate style to use. Just think of what churches would save on printed bulletins!

Instead, perhaps the most striking observation of biblical worship is its wealth of variety and few restrictions on form. Behold the vast wardrobe from which biblical worship is clothed!

Variety in Instruments

Harps (*Rev. 5:8*), stringed instruments (*Hab. 3:19*), horns, trumpets, loud-sounding cymbals, harps, lyres (*1 Chron. 15:28,29*), timbrels, tambourines (*Exod. 15:20*), gittith (a stringed instrument) (*Ps. 8*), instrument of ten strings (*Ps. 92:3*), pipe (*Ps. 150:4*), resounding cymbals (*Ps. 150:5*).

Variety of Volumes and Sounds

Loud (*Rev. 5:9*), like the sound of many waters, like the sound of loud thunder, like the sound of harpists (*Rev. 14:2*), voices accompanied by instruments (*2 Chron. 5:12-13*), shouting (*1 Chron. 15:28*), loud instruments (*2 Chron. 30:21*), a joyful noise (*Ps. 95:1*).

Variety of Worshipers

Appointed singers and musicians, trained by a skillful instructor (*1 Chron. 15:22*), organized by a chain of command (*1 Chron. 16:5; 25:6*), duet (*Judg. 5:1*), all the people of the land, led by singers and instruments (*2 Chron. 23:13*), everything that hath breath (*Ps. 150:6*).

Variety of Manner

Leaping, making merry (*1 Chron. 15:29*), clapping (*Ps. 47:1*), dancing (*Ex. 15:20*), lifting hands in the sanctuary (*Ps. 134:2*), appointed to worship (not spontaneous) (*2 Chron. 20:21*), guarded spontaniety (*1 Cor. 14*), by all the people, led by singers and instruments (*2 Chron. 23:13*), directed by leaders (*Neh. 12:46*).

Variety of Location

In the great congregation, in the house of the Lord (*1 Chron. 25:6*), on the walls of Jerusalem (*Neh. 12:31*), in the guest room of a house (*Mark 14:26*), coming down from a mountain (*1 Sam. 10:5-6*), in his mighty expanse, in his sanctuary (*Ps. 150:1*), in bed (*Ps. 149:5*), in jail (*Acts 16:25*).

Variety of Focus

Directed to the nations (*Ps. 117*), directed to one another (*Eph. 5:19*), directed to a troubled king (*1 Sam. 16:23*), directed to pagan kings (*Ps. 2*), directed to all the earth (*Ps. 100*), directed to God (*Ps. 138*).

Variety of Content

- Teaching or delineating truth: with much content (*Ps. 1, 119, 127*), with light reflections on one truth (*Ps. 133*).
- Prayer: opening the heart to God (*Ps. 131*),

petitioning for deliverance (*Ps. 3, 38*), with an emphasis on personal needs (*Ps. 6*), for vengeance on enemies (*Ps. 137*), confession, request for pardon (*Ps. 51*).

- Praise: for His wonderful works (*Ps. 8*), thanksgiving (*Ps. 138*), testimony of what God has done in personal life (*Ps. 18, 116*), testimony of what God has done in the life of a nation and history (*Ps. 78, 105*).
- Exhortation: to pagan kings (*Ps. 2*), to believers to bless the Lord (*Ps. 134*), to give thanks (*Ps. 136*), to hope in the Lord (*Ps. 131*).
- A profession of personal uprightness (*Ps. 101*).
- Using repetition (*Ps. 136* repeats the same phrase twenty-six times).

Variety of Occasions

The dedication of a wall (*Neh. 12:27*), going before an army (*2 Chron. 20:21*), accompanying offerings (*2 Chron. 23:18*), accompanying a feast (*2 Chron. 30:21*), the anointing of a king (*1 Kings 1:34*), during a new moon, during a full moon (*Ps. 81:3*), in a church service (*1 Cor. 14*), bringing up the ark of Solomon, eating the Passover supper (*Mark 14:26*), in a time of personal crisis (*Acts 16:25*).

Variety of Times of Day

Morning, evening (*1 Chron. 23:30*), night (*Ps. 92:2*), "from the rising of the sun to its setting" (*Ps. 113:3*).

Variety of Postures

Standing (*1 Chron. 23:30*), going before an army (*2 Chron. 20:21*), lifting hands (*Ps. 28:2*), bowing down, kneeling (*Ps. 95:6*).

Variety of Moods

Joy (*Ps. 33:1*), solemn sound on the harp (*Ps. 92:3*), chanting a lament (*2 Chron. 35:25*).

APPLICATIONS OF THE BIBLE ON FORM

From this survey of musical form, several implications concerning the present controversy can be noted. First, our creative Lord has allowed His creatures to exercise great creativity in worship. And God's Word does not even restrict us to the array of forms listed in the Bible.

In other words, folding one's hands while praying, though never mentioned in the Bible, should not be restricted for this reason. Additionally, if a culture deems a piano appropriate, and its use violates no biblical principle, we are apparently free to employ it for worship. God certainly never ordained that certain fixed forms should be rigidly followed week after week regardless of the culture. Could it be that we often misrepresent our creative Lord when we restrict ourselves to a few overused forms?

Second, several criticisms of contemporary Christian music are exposed as extrabiblical. For example, some critics deplore certain praise choruses that are theologically accurate but are not rich in theological depth when compared to, say, the works of Charles Wesley. And those who have followed in the steps of Wesley are to be commended for a tradition of hymns which have served the church well in teaching biblical theology.

But to snub a contemporary chorus because it merely relates a personal testimony of God's deliverance is not mature discernment, but unstudied prejudice. Many inspired psalms are by no means "theologically rich." Psalm 70 is simply a cry to God for help. Psalm 150 is an exhortation to praise God in various places and in various ways. Not every Christian song needs doctrinal depth to be useful for worship.

Critics should take care lest they find themselves in the uncomfortable position of having to explain how "And Can It Be" in all its theological profundity is superior to much of the inspired Psalter. Granted, there is a place for the hymns of Wesley, but to set his style as the standard by which all hymns are judged cannot be biblically justified.

If a song were written solely about how great it is when people get along with each other, would we consider this shallow? If so, we would demean Psalm 133. "Theologically rich" as a standard has the appearance of spiritual wisdom but is actually an attempt to be more spiritual than the Bible.

Others have posited rich harmony as a characteristic of all good music. But the Bible says nothing of rich harmony. If a certain cultural group deems this important, fine. But imposing it as a standard of good church music for all cultures at all times is certainly going beyond the Bible.

Still other arguments—such as: "The melody must be dominant"; "Songs should neither fade in nor fade out, but have a definite beginning and ending"; "Rhythm appeals to the body"—all must find their support outside the revealed Word of God.

But if such great diversity of forms are available, how do we decide which forms to use? Do we use variety for variety's sake, to keep the congregation guessing? Should we feel a responsibility to use all the aforementioned methods at some time during the church year? Should the minister choose what he likes best, regardless of tradition?

What if Jesse and his brothers offer to accompany a sacred number with their kazoos during the offertory? Would our rejection smack of cultural captivity as opposed to divine creativity?

These and other questions can be answered only as we study the functions of music in the Bible. Once we understand how music is to function in a given context, the form can be chosen that best aids this function.

FUNCTION IN MUSIC

Before we search the Scriptures for musical functions, two guiding principles should be laid out. First, whatever is commanded in the Bible will be considered normative. Second, since the Psalms are inspired songs, it would follow that their various functions are legitimate. So, using these two guiding principles, what functions of music do we find in the Scriptures?

As with form, we find that there are multiple functions of music presented in the Bible.

To Teach

Colossians 3:16 speaks of "teaching . . . one another with psalms and hymns, and spiritual songs." Psalm 27 and the hymns of Charles Wesley are excellent models of this function.

To Admonish

Again, Colossians 3:16 exhorts us to be "admonishing one another with psalms and hymns and spiritual songs." The Greek word *noutheteo* can be translated, "admonish, warn, instruct."[1] Colin Brown defines it this way: "to exert influence upon the will and decisions of another with the object of guiding into right behavior or encouraging to follow instruction."[2]

In other words, admonishing presupposes teaching and proceeds to urge one to follow this course. Wayward souls should be corrected, warned, and challenged by these songs to change their course. Examples in the Psalms include Psalm 131, which exhorts Israel to "hope in the Lord."

To Praise God

The Hebrew word *yadah* (as in Ps. 43:4) can be translated "to praise, confess, or give thanks."

The *Theological Wordbook of the Old Testament* defines it as a "public proclamation of God's attributes and His works."[3] As in our confession of sin we acknowledge or agree with God concerning our sin, in praise we confess God's attributes and works. Thanksgiving can be included in praise. It is a way of praising. Psalm 8 praises God for his wonderful works. Psalm 138 gives thanks for his character and deeds.

To Confess Sin to God

Psalm 51 expresses a sinner's confession of sin and prayer for pardon.

To Make a Petition to God

(*Psalm 3*)

To Relate a Personal Testimony

(*Psalm 116*)

Are these the only legitimate functions of music? God never set these boundaries in his Word, so what right have I to speak for God in denying a function that he never prohibited?

Singing "Happy Birthday" at a party, playing in a high school band, or composing an instrumental piece for the sheer enjoyment of the music may not be specifically commended in Scripture, but neither is it condemned.[4]

And what of our evangelistic hymnody, which has been attacked as sub-biblical by some? Again, although the evangelistic use of music may not be specifically alluded to in Scripture, this function is never condemned. And since the apostle Paul sought to use all legitimate means (1 Cor. 9:22) to see people saved, surely history teaches that music is one of the most powerful means of evangelism, when accompanied by anointed preaching.

Even in a church service, Paul recognized the presence of unbelievers and indicated that they should be considered in planning worship activities (see 1 Cor. 14:22-25). Should we not consider the unbeliever as we select our music?

Further, perhaps the gospel song could also be seen as teaching (how to be saved) or admonishing (the need to be saved), functions that are clearly stated in Colossians. Whatever the case, those who decry the evangelistic function of music are going beyond the Scriptures.

ON SELECTING MUSIC

But back to the minister and his quandary with the kazoo band. Although a multitude of musical forms are available for our use, not all will best serve the intended function of the offertory. Is the intent to draw the hearts of worshipers to praise God from their hearts? If so, the kazoo band would probably fail. Save them for a potluck supper.

Perhaps a choir special focusing on the Lord's greatness would function well for this offertory. A beautiful organ solo, if the tune is familiar, could direct the worshipers' minds as the text is recalled. If unfamiliar, the solo would probably draw attention to the music and the performer rather than the Lord, and again the intended function of praise would be unfulfilled.

This is not to say that an unfamiliar organ solo is bad in itself or should never be used. But in a segment of a service designed for praise, the function must determine the form.

Thus, when wrestling with decisions concerning form, it would seem that *the form should always be subservient to and determined by the intended function in a particular context.* We must constantly ask why we are doing what we are doing. Albert Einstein has well stated, "Perfection of means and confusion of ends seem to characterize our age."[5] All too often this deficiency characterizes our use of music in the church.

How often do we choose certain hymns solely because we like the tunes, train our choirs in a style solely because it is traditional, or restrict our range of forms to the musical taste of the leaders? Rather, we need to determine our goals and choose the forms that best aid us in achieving those goals.

Charles Wesley wrote many hymns to teach biblical theology to the common person. Whereas much of the preaching of that day was far over the head of many of the common folk, his hymns put the Bible on a lower shelf accessible to all. Many of today's praise choruses, attested by many as functioning well in the context of praise, would have missed Wesley's target.

Similarly, D. L. Moody's driving passion was

evangelism. When he searched for a song leader for his meetings, he didn't ask the local conservatory of music for the most proficient musician and soloist. Rather, he looked for a person whose singing and leading could touch the hearts of the lost and wayward.

Many trained singers, proficient in the style of the opera, could have outperformed Ira Sankey. But Moody's goal was not to get raving reviews from the press or to upgrade the masses' appreciation of fine music. He wanted to see souls saved. God used Ira Sankey and his unique ability to "sing the gospel" in one of the world's most effective evangelistic efforts.

In the evangelistic settings encountered by Moody, the music of Sankey reached the common person in a way that Bach never could. According to historian Paul Lang, in Bach's later years even his own congregation in Leipzig could not comprehend his music.[6] Stevenson notes that a four-month campaign in England found Sankey singing to over 2 million people. By way of contrast, "it is an open question . . . whether 2,500,000 persons as an aggregate total listened to actual performances of such masterworks of Bach as his passions or his masses during the entire 19th century."[7] "*Salvation and Solos* [Sankey's songbook] has undoubtedly 'saved' millions. Whether any composition of Bach, on the other hand, has ever brought even a single person to the altar for a confession of sin or into the inquiry room for pastoral prayer is doubtful."[8]

From the perspective of "serious" music critics, Bach's works are far superior to Sankey's. And undoubtedly many have been drawn closer to God by their exposure to the music of Bach. But for the people Moody was targeting, and to fulfill the function of evangelizing them, Sankey's music proved superior.

Should we then all flock to the songs of Sankey when pursuing evangelism? Not necessarily. His gospel songs functioned well in America and a few European countries during the late 1800s. Today we must evaluate our own culture as to which forms will best fulfill such functions as evangelizing the lost, teaching and admonishing believers, praising and praying to the Father, and wishing a child a happy birthday.

8

Biblical Principles for Musicians and Sponsors

Thy Word is a lamp to my feet, and a light to my path.

Psalm 119:105

A powerful tool must be used in a proper way. In the hands of the master chef, a gas flame is used to prepare a feast. In the hands of the ignorant, the same flame can be dangerous. Controlled by the arsonist, the flame becomes deadly.

Likewise with contemporary Christian music: if biblical principles are violated, using this tool can be meaningless, divisive, or destructive, even when the music is used with the best intentions. In this chapter, we will go beyond Scripture's specific teachings on music to consider more general scriptural principles that impact our *use* of music, whether our position be that of worship leader, promoter, performer, or missionary.

BECOME ALL THINGS TO ALL PEOPLE
This scriptural principle from 1 Corinthians 9:19-

23 shows that we must choose styles understood by the targeted culture. It is in this section of the Scripture that the apostle Paul revealed a key component of his evangelistic strategy when he stated, "I have become all things to all men, that I may by all means save some." As we discussed in chapter 3, when targeting Jews, Paul became as a Jew. He observed their laws, although he was free from the law, in order to reach the Jews. When targeting Gentiles, his method changed so that his message of grace would not be obscured by the appearance of legalism. So while his message was firm, his methods were flexible. The determining factor was the cultural heritage of his target group.

Now, let us apply this principle to questions regarding musical style. How can we become all things to all people regarding our music?

First, we must resign ourselves to the fact that no single form of music will function equally well in all cultural contexts. We dare not base our decisions concerning musical forms on what has worked in the past, what ministers to us, or what seems appropriate from our unique cultural heritage. If decisions are made on these bases, we reverse the Pauline principle. We make the target group become all things to us, requiring them to cross a cultural barrier to get saved or to grow in Jesus.

Paul did just the opposite. He was consistent with the example of the Son of God in his incarnation. In other words, Paul left his own comfort zone, the cultural heritage with which he felt comfortable, in order to reach others with methods more comfortable to them. So to follow the biblical precedent we must know our target group and, ultimately, rely on the spiritually minded individuals of that group to judge what is most effective among their people.

Is long hair inappropriate for a male singer? Is a skirt on a man an indication of transvestism? Is a large choir the best medium for reverential worship? The answers to these questions may, on the surface, seem obvious, yet a shift in culture can reverse the response. John Wesley wore long hair, which was appropriate for his culture. First-century Roman soldiers wore skirts, and no one would dare call them feminine! We may enjoy choirs performing traditional hymns, but some Africans deem our traditional hymns inappropriate for a worship service. Why? Because the hymns sound like their funeral songs.[1]

"Then which church music is the best church music?" we might ask. Paul might have responded, "Give me your target group and your intended function within the group, and we will decide." Are you planning an evangelistic dinner for a cultured group of upper-middle-class adults in New York? Perhaps an evening of Bach and the testimony of a performer would function well. Are you leading worship at a summer conference for teens? Doug Couch of the Youth Evangelism Department of the Georgia Baptist Convention conducts a summer youth conference that attracts over six thousand teens each year. For this event, he lines up song leaders that sing high-energy music and use acoustic guitars or electric keyboards. This effectively draws the kids into worship and prepares them for the spoken Word. Groups such as Truth and New Song also perform each week. The fruit of this ministry is impressive.

Are you working with inner-city kids? Try a Resurrection Band concert for the hard rockers or a Christian rap group for those who prefer that style. Are you working with children? Al Menconi listened to a Christian album and lamented that it had "the spiritual depth of a ten-year-old." But before disposing of the album, it occurred to him that he had a ten-year-old daughter. He gave it to her. She loved it![2]

The accessibility of radios, cassette tapes, and CDs has led to such a wide range of popular styles that predicting the effectiveness of a style for even one strata of a society—say, the American teenager—is not a simple process. Some teens prefer country music and would be disgusted with the music of Petra. Others prefer rock and put down country as "hick music." Some respond positively to Amy Grant; others view her music as wimpy. It is really quite amazing how youth can be at once so critical of adults who don't understand their music and so demeaning to fellow youth who enjoy a different style from their own. In music ministry, the difference between a good group and just the right group can be "the difference between lightning and a lightning bug."

For the minister concerned with giving a clear presentation of the gospel, a thorough under-standing of the target group's musical preference is essential. To ignore such cultural nuances is to risk presenting Jesus as irrelevant, or even "wimpy."

FIT THE MUSIC TO THE OCCASION

Within every cultural group, there are musical forms appropriate for some occasions that are inappropriate for others. Proverbs 25:20 puts it this way: "Like one who takes off a garment on a cold day, or like vinegar on soda, is he who sings songs to a troubled heart" (see also Amos 6:5).

The ideal music for a singles banquet may raise eyebrows in a formal worship service. Likewise, music that would stir the hearts of an older audi-ence quite probably would bore a teenage audience to tears. Insensitivity to such cultural subtleties can thwart the intended impact of a well-meaning wor-ship planner.

PREPARE DILIGENTLY

The high caliber of musical entertainment that con-stantly is paraded before the Western world has spoiled the public. Secular musicians take their per-formances seriously, expending great effort to pro-duce just the right sound, fit the peculiar acoustics of the concert hall, and execute the performance flawlessly. Many concerts are an astounding display of music, light, and technoelectronic wonders. It is no surprise that many people are bored in church worship services.

Sadly, non-Christians have often taken musical excellence more seriously than the church. While the world has become accustomed to musical professionalism, all too often the church has remained, as Franky Schaeffer put it, "addicted to mediocrity." Paul expressed the biblical standard in his letter to the Colossians: "Whatever you do, do your work heartily, as for the Lord rather than for men" (Col. 3:23). Biblical commentator R. C. H. Lenski paraphrases this verse: "Throw your soul into the work as if your one employer were the Lord!"[3] But all too often, as someone once said, Christians "worship their work, work at their play, and play at their worship."

Christian musicians, and those involved in Christian music ministry, must even go beyond just a commitment to musical excellence. They must devote themselves to the work of prayer. To adapt a quote of Samuel Chadwick: "Satan laughs at our toil, mocks at our musicianship, but trembles when we pray."

FOCUS ON GOD AND OTHERS

Music's popularity poses the threat of luring big egos that are hungry for gratification. Christian musicians must fight the temptation to substitute stardom for servanthood. This is one area where the Bible is clear: "God is opposed to the proud, but gives grace to the humble" (1 Pet. 5:5). M. R. Vincent notes that the word *opposed*, used in this Scripture verse, is a "strong and graphic word. Lit[erally], setteth Himself in array against, as one draws out a host for battle."[4]

Pride is a serious sin. The godly promoter will find ways to distinguish between the star and the servant, taking care to book only musicians who wish to serve as positive role models, not to be worshiped as heroes. Some of the most effective ministry that takes place at a concert is accomplished after the performance, when weary band members give of themselves to those needing spiritual counsel or just offer a warm embrace and a listening ear. The mature band understands that ultimate success is not measured by the number of tapes sold but by the number of people who are served (see Matt. 23:11).

A caution should be heeded at this point. Some manifestations of pride—such as requiring high-class accommodations, constant complaining, or shunning the lowly—are easy to spot. A spectacular light show or flashy stage presence may or may not reveal pride. Perhaps a humble servant is simply attempting to "become all things to all men" in order to reach a group of people who consider lasers and stage fog appropriate to the medium. For many serious concert-goers, a performance with static lighting and immobile band members sends a message that the band is not excited about their message.

Again, the communicative value of such trappings is best determined by the target audience. An adult may denounce a Petra concert as "too showy," but how does the target audience, the youth, evaluate it? Perhaps only they can accurately assess whether the stage show enhanced or hindered the worship of God, the edification of the believer, or the evangelization of the lost.

It is difficult, if not impossible, for us to judge a person's sincerity of heart. During a guitar solo, one musician may be looking for the applause of people. If that is the case, no matter how many lives are touched, he has received his reward in full (see Matt. 6:2). Another musician plays his solo to the glory of God, knowing that whether the audience applauds the group and repents before God or remains stiff-necked and wants nothing of the group or their God, he has given of his best to the Master, looking to the Lord alone for his praise. He knows that one day he will hear the blessed words: "Well done, thou good and faithful servant" (Matt. 25:21).

> *Therefore do not go on passing judgment before the time, but wait until the Lord comes, who will both bring to light the things hidden in the darkness and disclose the motives of men's hearts; and then each man's praise will come to him from God. (1 Cor. 4:5)*

DEVELOP ACCOUNTABILITY
In recent years many highly visible Christian lead-

ers have been involved in scandals that brought disgrace to the church. Perhaps much of this could have been avoided if these leaders had placed themselves under authority. The Evangelical Council for Financial Accountability oversees the finances of many Christian organizations. Music ministries would do well to establish both spiritual and financial accountability, as some are doing already. Mylon LeFevre serves with Broken Heart Ministries under the wing of Mount Paran Church of God in metro Atlanta. Amy Grant and Michael W. Smith receive visits from their pastors prior to some of their performances.

With many hours logged on the road away from their local church, traveling ministers must find ways to develop accountability and work under authority. The author of Hebrews admonishes us: "Obey your leaders, and submit to them; for they keep watch over your souls, as those who will give an account" (Heb. 13:17).

DEMAND SPIRITUAL QUALIFICATIONS

All too often bands are booked solely because someone likes their music. If songs are to be used as an avenue for teaching (Col. 3:16), should not the warning of James 3:1 apply to singers as well as preachers? "Let not many of you become teachers, my brethren, knowing that as such we shall incur a stricter judgment." If so, then the ability to sing is only one qualification for someone who wishes to minister through song.

Before a church hires a minister of music or books a band, some hard questions must be addressed. If musicians are considered visible servants or leaders within the church, shouldn't they exhibit the qualifications of elders or deacons as listed in 1 Timothy 3 and Titus 1? Singers' lives should be congruous with their lyrics.

The good musician who is not spiritually qualified may nullify the message he is singing with what one sees in his life. Or suppose a vocalist is asked to sing to a group that God wants to rebuke for its spiritual bankruptcy? Only the minister filled with God's Spirit and power could discern the Spirit's leading and exhibit the fortitude to deliver such an unpopular message.

Secular musicians may judge their success by applause and record sales. But men and women of God must abandon themselves to the will of God, making themselves available to deliver God's message for the occasion. For them, the success of a worship service is not determined solely by the question, Did the congregation enjoy it? Their main concern is, Did God enjoy it?

Going beyond the qualifications of good musicianship, we should ask such questions as: Do the musicians want to get rich? (See 1 Tim. 3:3 and 6:9-10.) Do they have a good reputation? (See 1 Tim. 3:2.) Are they new Christians? (See 1 Tim. 3:6.) Is their doctrine pure? (See 1 Tim. 3:9 and Tit. 1:9.) Do their lyrics qualify as proper objects of meditation? (See Phil. 4:8.)

Finally, examine the fruit of the lives of those who seek to minister through music. In the context of dealing with false prophets, Jesus instructed the multitudes, "You will know them by their fruits" (Matt. 7:20). We should expose our flock only to those ministries that have a good track record regarding the fruit of their labors. A false prophet may very well sing like an angel, but God's Word indicates that the quality of the voice should never be the sole determiner of the legitimacy of a ministry. We owe it to our congregations to dig deeper.

STRIVE TO COMMUNICATE

Paul's request for prayer in Colossians 4:3-4 should be echoed by every performer and worship leader: "that God may open a door for our message, so that we may proclaim the mystery of Christ, for which I am in chains. Pray that I may proclaim it clearly, as I should" (NIV).

Clarity of message through song is no simple matter, especially in a concert hall. Even when singers do their best to clearly enunciate their words, messages can be obscured through acoustical flaws, resulting in echoes or other distortions. Secular artists can rest assured that their fans know the words well enough from radio and cassettes to appreciate their live music, even in less than ideal conditions. But for the local youth minister, seeking to bring the lost to hear a band with which they are unfamiliar, the problem of clarity becomes acute, particularly with heavier rock styles.

Often the lack of clarity caused by the variables of a concert can be overcome by the foresight of the local church promoter. One way to alleviate the problem is to find out which songs will be played (through the group's home office) and play these songs (via cassette) with overheads of the words in a youth meeting several days prior to the concert. Another way is to make tapes available to those unfamiliar with the group. In places where English is a second language, one band projects the lyrics on the screen to ensure communication.

Of course, the problem of clarity is not unique to the rock genre. As has been noted, some of Bach's music was not understood by his own congregation. Similarly, much opera is hard for the uninitiated to interpret. This does not make these forms substandard. It may just mean that for many some preparation would enhance the impact of the performance.

BE SENSITIVE TO THE WEAK

It is one thing to share the truth but often quite another to share the truth in love. Those who use contemporary Christian music must consider those who have been carefully guarded from any contemporary forms of music, being convinced of the music's inherently evil nature. Others to consider would be those who have been saved out of a secular rock subculture, from which they want to stay as far away as possible. Like any other controversial subject, we must exercise sensitivity toward those who may never understand the use of such forms for the Lord.

Those who mistakenly believe a neutral practice is sinful are labeled "weak" by the apostle Paul. To better understand the appropriate response to the weak, let us take Romans 14 and substitute the issue of listening to music:

> *Now accept the one who is weak in faith, but not for the purpose of passing judgment on his opinions. One man has faith that he may listen to contemporary Christian music, but he who is weak listens to traditional Christian music only. Let not him who listens to contemporary Christian music regard with contempt him who does not listen to contemporary Christian music, and let not him who does not listen to contemporary Christian music judge him who listens to contemporary Christian music, for God has accepted him. . . . Therefore let us not judge one another anymore, but rather determine this—not to put an obstacle or stumbling block in a brother's way.*

PART THREE

A REVEALING JOURNEY THROUGH HISTORY

9

FROM EARLY CHANTS TO REFORMATION SONGS

At the crossroads on the path that leads to the future, tradition has placed against each of us ten thousand men to guard the past.
Belgian philosopher Maurice Maeterlinck

"Someone's got to take a stand!" the wealthy churchman must have thought. "The church should be a place of purity and holiness, separate from the world and its secular entertainment. How could good Christians conceive of welcoming this worldly instrument into the Lord's house?" The churchman did all that he could to thwart the efforts of the "misguided" group that had conceded to accept the sinister gift, beseeching them with tears and even offering to refund the entire price if someone would only dump the ill-fated cargo—a musical instrument—overboard during its transatlantic voyage.

Just what was this instrument of such vile associations and shady history that it elicited such opposition? The electric guitar or drums? Hardly. The churchman's pleas were left unheeded; the instrument arrived safely in the New World, and the Brattle Street Church of Boston made room for the controversial instrument: the organ.[1]

Our century is far from alone in its witness to the introduction of secular forms into sacred song. In fact, as we shall see, many of the hymns considered traditional today were revolutionary at their inception. We dare not deal with the present controversy in isolation from similar musical changes that have occurred through the centuries. Otherwise, we risk repeating the mistakes of the past and reaping the consequences.

In this chapter we will discover answers to the following important questions: Where did our traditional hymns originate? How have people reacted to innovations in sacred music through the years? Is today's controversy following a historical pattern? Is the practice of adopting the styles of popular secular music a twentieth-century innovation? When the musical styles of the church and the world begin to overlap, is the outcome positive or negative in the long run? Is new hymnody important in times of renewal? The historical precedents that we uncover could well prove to be the most fascinating and enlightening aspect of the present controversy.

Let's look for the answers to these and other intriguing questions as we distance ourselves from the present controversy and embark upon a fascinating journey through church history, stopping only at those junctures where new musical forms are introduced.

THE CHANTS OF THE EARLY AND MEDIEVAL CHURCH

The cultural milieu of the early church was primarily Greek rather than Hebrew. Jewish synagogues were scattered among the main population centers, but Greek thought and art forms dominated those early centuries. Thus the New Testament was written in Greek rather than Hebrew, and the ancient hymnwriters set their lyrics to music with its stylistic roots in pagan Greek culture rather than biblical Hebrew culture.[2] During the second century, Gnostics and Arians wrote hymns to propagate their heretical teachings, and these hymns obtained a wide circulation. By the fourth century these were some of the most popular hymns. Ephraem Syrus (307–373), a distinguished father of the Syrian church, countered by writing hymns to champion orthodoxy. But rather than create a new, sacred style in which to couch the truth, he opted to use the same meters as the popular Gnostic songs and thus exerted a powerful influence.

This introduced a great era of hymnody in both Syriac and Greek.[3] Early Latin hymns had a similar background. As David Breed put it, Hilary of Poiters, in the fourth century, "Was incited by the singing of the Arians . . . to write similar songs for the propagation of the orthodox faith."[4]

The music of these songs consisted of a one-part chant based on the four principal Greek modes. Although certain modes used in the heathen temples and theaters were forbidden in the church, the adopted modes found their origins in the pagan Greek civilization.

According to Donald Paul Ellsworth, "During the first centuries, the church continually borrowed secular musical sources and practices." [5] There was no further development in style until Pope Gregory the Great (590–604) modified the scales and produced what became known as the Gregorian chant.[6] All voices sang in unison, all musical instruments were restricted, and only men were allowed to sing in worship.[7]

Once Gregorian chant became firmly entrenched in the church, changes from this now "sacred" style were resisted. Pope John XII (c. 1324) issued a decree by which "any means of composition which expressed contemporary secular art" would be rejected. According to Karl Gustav Fellerer in *The History of Catholic Church Music,* "New means of composition would be acceptable only after they had been tried and had lost their force in contemporary secular music. . . . This was to be the viewpoint of the church for centuries."[8] Thus the medieval church resolved to remain a step behind the world in its musical development. This approach certainly succeeded in keeping church music separate from the world's popular music, but one wonders if, in the process, worship lost its relevance to the common person. As we near the Reformation era, we find rumblings that this is indeed the case—and we find religious mavericks who begin to use the popular music of their culture.

MARTIN LUTHER AND THE REFORMATION

Even before Christianity came to Germany, the German people were avid singers. The common people had legions of songs to accompany their festivals and praise their heathen deities.[9] After their conversion to Catholicism, they began composing their own hymns outside the church, couching their religious lyrics in the old familiar tunes that were remnants of their pre-Christian days. In addition, they translated the Latin hymns of the Roman church into their common language, added original tunes, and sang their praises outside the established church at their festivals and pilgrimages. The Bohemians, Moravians, and followers of John Huss put such an emphasis on popular praise that in 1504 a hymnbook was published for use by the congregation.[10] Praise was again in the language and style of the common person, but without the blessing of the Roman Catholic church. It remained for Martin Luther and the Reformation to make a break from the established church and give full expression to the new hymnody.

In July of 1505, Luther, as a young law student, had a brush with death in a thunderstorm. This event led him to vow to become a monk. However, after coming to an evangelical view of justification by faith through his study of Romans, he protested against major abuses of the Roman church in his Ninety-five Theses. Many German people rallied behind him. The papacy countered, and the Reformation was on.

But Reformed theology was not the only interest of the great reformer. Luther was also vitally interested in reforming the worship of the church, putting it into the language of the common person. For him, music was more than just a warm-up to a sermon. Luther wrote about the centrality of music in a letter dated October 4, 1530:

> I really believe, nor am I shamed to assert, that next to theology there is no art equal to music. . . . Praising music is like trying to paint a great subject on a small canvas, which turns out merely a daub. But my love for it abounds; it has often refreshed me and freed me from great troubles.[11]

Again, he said, "Music is a noble gift of God, next to theology. I would not change my little knowledge of music for a great deal."[12] And still again, "Experience proves that next to the Word of God only music deserves to be extolled as the mistress and governess of the feelings of the human heart."[13]

Because of his high view of music, Luther himself played the lute and the flute, often singing at the table and composing hymns for the church. He also urged educators to teach children music in their earliest years. As for teachers and pastors, he categorically stated, "A schoolmaster must be able to sing, or I will not look at him; nor should one admit young men to the ministry unless they have practiced and studied music at school."[14]

Luther's thrust in worship was to make it appealing to the simple, common folk. Concerning the daily worship service he stated, "It is best that such a service be planned for the young and for the unlearned folk who come to church."[15]

In order to make hymns appealing he urged, "Please omit all new-fangled court expressions, for to win popularity a song must be in the most simple and common language."[16] Thus, Luther's songs consisted of commonplace expressions that the common, unsophisticated German could easily comprehend. The models for his lyrics were the popular ballads of his day.[17] The tunes were borrowed from the German folk songs, the music of the masses, and even a hymn to Mary.[18] Luther was not so concerned with the associations or origins of the tunes as he was with their ability to communicate truth.

> *He could not and would not think of destroying or putting aside everything he found. . . . Whatever could be given a new label and laden with the power of the gospel could also serve to propagate this message and make it drive even deeper into men's hearts and expand throughout the state and the country.*[19]

Luther marveled that in secular art there were "so many beautiful songs, while in the religious field we have such rotten, lifeless stuff." He concluded, "The devil has no need of all the good tunes for himself," and proceeded to release these tunes from their secular or unbiblical words and unite them with words consistent with the evangelical faith. He compiled a German mass in 1526, directing its appeal to the youth. "For the youth's sake," wrote Luther, "we must read, sing, preach, write, and compose verse, and whenever it was helpful and beneficial I would let all the bells peal, all the organs thunder, and everything sound that could sound."[20]

Luther cared only about music's ability to communicate biblical truth and to set on fire the hearts of people. And set a fire he did. Thirty-six church hymns, including "A Mighty Fortress Is Our God," have been ascribed to Luther, although most of these, as previously noted, were expanded or revised from preexisting material.[21] The wedding of popular styles with understandable, evangelical lyrics proved to be a healthy marriage. Luther's hymns "were carried from place to place in the form of leaflets, or were sung in towns and villages by wandering minstrels. Memorized by young and old throughout Germany, they paved the way for the Reformation."[22]

These heartfelt hymns carried the Reformation message to places where Luther's words alone may have never penetrated. In Tilemann Heshusius's introduction to the Psalms of David, he wrote, "I do not doubt that the one song of Luther, 'Ye Christians One and All Rejoice,' brought many hundreds of Christians a new faith, who heretofore did not want to hear the name Luther mentioned. But the dear words of Luther did win their hearts and they had to follow the truth."[23]

Even Luther's enemies had to acknowledge the impact. Jesuit Adam Conzenius lamented, "Luther's hymns have destroyed more souls than his writings and speeches."[24] A Spanish monk, Thomas à Jesu, noted, "It is surprising how those hymns spread Lutheranism. Written in German, they literally flew out of Luther's study, landing in homes, in places of work, and were sung in the markets, in the streets, and on the field."[25]

Such was the power of the hymns that spoke the language of the common person. And Luther was not alone in his methodology of borrowing from the popular music of his day. Others adopted his view, and in a 1574 letter to Frederick III of Saxony, the seniors of the Bohemian Brethren wrote of their songbook: "Our melodies have been adapted from secular songs, and foreigners have at times objected. But our singers have taken into consideration the fact that the people are more easily persuaded to accept the truth by songs whose melodies are well known to them."[26]

But not everyone concurred with Luther's approach to hymnody. In addition to Catholic censure, some fellow reformers voted thumbs down to this marriage of Catholic or secular music with Reformation texts. In 1524 Zwingli reacted against using any instruments that had associations with the Catholic church.[27] However, it was the opposition of John Calvin to the hymns and instruments that proved to be the most enduring.

JOHN CALVIN AND THE METRICAL PSALM

John Calvin (1509–1564) felt that instruments were tolerated in Old Testament times only because the people of God were in their infancy. He believed that the best praise was simple and from the heart. Thus he opposed the use of instruments and singing in parts. In addition, he censured the singing of any lyrics not found in the Scriptures, allowing only the inspired psalms to be sung in worship.[28]

The churches of Geneva—as well as many in Scotland and England—by and large followed Calvin, repressing many artistic elements as remnants of the papacy. The people felt so strongly that their view was the biblical view that decrees were issued and many church organs were destroyed. The metrical psalms exercised such a wide influence that they became the exclusive church music in many churches for more than a hundred years.[29]

But where did this psalm singing originate? Were all of their origins distinctly spiritual? In the first half of the sixteenth century, Clement Marot of France, the court poet of King Francis I, began to write metrical versions of the Psalms.[30] These were set to popular French tunes and were sung, not so much as an act of worship but as a delightful art, to the accompaniment of the viol or flute.

These psalms eventually became so popular and

effective in spreading the Reformation doctrine
that, after publishing a volume of the metrical
psalms in 1542, Marot was forced to seek refuge in
Geneva. In 1562 a complete edition of the *Geneva
Psalter* was published at the request of Calvin. One
of the musicians who set the Psalms to music, Louis
Bourgeois, was in charge of music at the Huguenot
church in Geneva under Calvin. Bourgeois and
another musician set the Psalms,

> *to airs drawn from popular melodies of the
> time, and this psalter became a store of song
> for the people. The psalms were heard in castle
> and cottage. They were sung by workers in the
> fields and the mills, they were the first lessons
> imparted to children, and frequently became
> the last words heard on the lips of the dying.*[31]

The *Geneva Psalter* was translated and widely
circulated in France, Switzerland, Germany, Holland, and Denmark.[32] A similar movement produced an English psalter. Yet, during the time of
their introduction, Calvin's popular psalm-tunes
were not universally well received. Some people
even scorned them as "Geneva Jiggs."[33] Yet these
tunes became authorized, and to meddle with them
was no trifling matter.[34] Louis Bourgeois was
arrested and imprisoned in 1551 for changing the
melodies of certain psalms without permission.
Remember Bourgeois? He was the man who had
set the Psalms to the original tunes years earlier![35]

Over the years these tunes had become identified with church worship, and the resulting sentiment was well expressed by an old family servant who vowed she would "sing the Psalms of David to the tunes of David and nothing else."[36] The passage of time had bestowed a sacred status on the once secular tunes. Man's tunes had now become God's tunes.

10

FROM PSALM SINGING TO HYMNODY

Those who cannot remember the past are condemned to repeat it.

Santayana

Chapter 9 left us with two divergent streams of church (sacred) music: Germany followed Luther's lead in singing hymns, while Protestants in England and Scotland followed Calvin in restricting themselves to psalm singing. The conversion of these countries to the hymn did not come easily. Innovators who tried to write hymns met with considerable resistance.

John Bunyan's attempt to introduce hymns resulted in the split of his own church. In 1691, after his death, the church finally reached a compromise. Those consciously opposed to the hymn could either sit through the hymn singing in silence or remain in the vestibule until that portion of the service was over.[1] Benjamin Keach began advocating hymns among the Particular Baptists in 1673. Although initially he was violently attacked by members of his own group, by

1690 his congregation was singing hymns every Sunday.

Despite these isolated steps forward, hymn singing was still frowned upon by the church at large.[2] Some further impetus was needed to secure a more general acceptance. It would be Isaac Watts who, more than any other person, would open the floodgates for the introduction of the hymn.

ISAAC WATTS

Near the close of the seventeenth century, the traditional psalm singing was, for many, no longer providing a fresh worship. In part, the problem was inherent in the nature of the metrical psalm. When the biblical psalm was forced into rhyme and meter, while strictly adhering to the content of the original psalm, the resulting poetry was often awkward. [3] As a result, the poetry of these psalms had little appeal, especially to those who appreciated fine literature and poetry.[4]

Watts certainly was well acquainted with the literature of his time, having studied Hebrew at the age of thirteen, French at ten, Greek at nine, and Latin at four! At age twenty he returned home after his schooling and complained to his father about the uncouth psalm versions used in their services. His father responded by challenging him to compose something better. Young Isaac took him seriously and wrote his first hymn, "Behold the Glories of the Lamb."[5]

He went on to write over 750 hymns and

psalms[6] and had such an initial impact and enduring influence that he has been deemed the "Father of English Hymnody." Included in his hymns are many that are still cherished today, such as "O God, Our Help in Ages Past," "Joy to the World!" "Alas! and Did My Savior Bleed?" "I Sing the Mighty Power of God," "Jesus Shall Reign Where'er the Sun," and "When I Survey the Wondrous Cross."

Watts's hymnwriting was tempered by the tenacity with which parishioners held to singing the psalms. Thus he deemed it necessary to tie his hymns closely enough to the psalms to be designated as such. Yet he took the liberty of straying so far from the original content of the psalms as to bring in New Testament themes. His desire was to harness and use the appeal of good poetry. Instead of producing ornate songs for the literary sophisticate, he sought to produce songs for the edification of the simplest worshiper.[7]

The psalm singing of Watts's day was not functioning to direct hearts and minds to God in worship. Rather, it was putting people to sleep. In a letter to Isaac Watts, his brother Enoch admitted his opinion of their church's worship: "But Mason now reduces this kind of writing to a sort of yawning indifference, and honest Barton *[Barton's Psalter]* chimes us to sleep. There is, therefore, great need of a [pen], vigorous and lively as yours, to quicken and revive the dying devotion of our age, to which nothing can afford such assistance as poetry, contrived on purpose to elevate us above ourselves."[8]

So Watts took up his "vigorous and lively pen," harnessed the tool of poetry, and began a reformation in Christian worship.

But tradition doesn't relinquish its grip easily. One source of conflict was the attitude that poetry was too worldly an art to be used in the church. According to Watts, the poetry of his time was "enslaved to vice and profaneness" and had "so far lost the memory of its birthplace as to be engaged in the interests of hell!"[9] Some had seen poetry used exclusively in secular settings and so could not imagine it being used in church music.

As Watts himself put it, "They will venture to sing a dull hymn or two at church, in tunes of equal dullness; but they still persuade themselves . . . that the beauties of poetry are vain and dangerous."[10] But for Watts, poetry was not evil in itself. It was just a tool that had been used for and associated with evil. It was not beyond the redeeming hand of God and so could be used profitably for God.

The second source of attack came from those who cherished the traditional psalm singing and recognized that Watts had strayed far from a strict adherence to the original psalms. This sentiment was expressed by William Romaine in 1755 when he asked: "Why should Watts, or any hymnmaker, not only take the precedence of the Holy Ghost, but also thrust him entirely out of the church?"[11]Romaine further complained that

"Christian congregations [had] shut out divinely inspired Psalms" and had "taken in Dr. Watts's flights of fancy."[12] And from another critic, "The rhymes of a man are now magnified above the Word of God."[13]

Churches split, pastors were ousted, and some people were so enraged that, in retrospect, the conflict took on almost comical proportions. In the mid-eighteenth century, some of British general Wolfe's troops, stationed in Aberdeen, heartily sang hymns at a church parade in the cathedral. The local folk were so impressed that they hired one of the men to become the singing master for the city parishes. As students from the university attended the cathedral, they would join heartily in singing the hymns. Consequently hymn singing grew in popularity.

There was one group of people, however, who detested this innovation to such an extent that they, according to historian H. A. L. Jefferson, "hired three young urchins with shrill voices to sit on the pulpit steps and sing lustily out of tune," assisted by one Gideon Duncan. The service ended in chaos, with the "slow singers" and "quick singers" contesting one another. "The unruly boys were given a sound thrashing, while the unfortunate Duncan was hauled before the magistrate for singing out of tune, being fined £50 and imprisoned until it was paid."[14] (Looking for an innovative fund-raiser? Try fining those of *your* congregation who sing off-key!)

Understandably the hymn was slow in achieving

a large measure of acceptance, but when it did, the roots of tradition again quickly set in and the lessons of the past were forgotten. Consequently some independent churches resisted the introduction of any new hymns, other than those of Watts, just as forcefully as Watts's hymns had been resisted years earlier![15]

In passing, it should be noted that not all of Watts's hymns were of the quality of those that have survived the scrutiny of time. What we sing today is a distillation of the best hymns of the past several hundred years, the weak and errant being, by and large, rooted out. Some of Watts's hymns changed the original intent of the Psalms to glorify his country. For example, the last part of Psalm 107 was entitled: "Colonies planted; or nations blest and punish'd; a Psalm for New England."[16] His poems on the theme of divine love were too sensual for many to accept. John Wesley spoke of these poems as offending "in a more grotesque manner, than in anything which was before published in the English tongue."[17]

Whenever new hymnody flourishes, some of the hymns will be of poor quality, but this should not drive us to reject all that is offered. As the father of English hymnody, the best of Watts's songs have endured for almost three centuries and are still some of the most beloved hymns of the church.

CHARLES WESLEY
Charles Wesley was born in 1707 in Epworth,

England, into a time when religion was at a low
ebb. Immorality in high places was not disgraced;
drunkenness was not frowned upon, and the
church was lifeless.[18] Into this decadent culture
God breathed renewal, and to a large extent his
instruments were John and Charles Wesley. In stark
contrast to the cold formality of the church, the
Wesleys preached and sang about a vibrant relationship with a personal God, and hearts were revital-
ized. A great spiritual movement, Methodism,
began—a movement in which the new hymnody of
Charles Wesley played a vital role.

Although Watts and others had introduced the
hymn earlier, the Psalms still reigned supreme in
most English congregations until the early years of
the nineteenth century. As late as 1819 a lawsuit was
brought against a clergyman who sought to introduce a book containing hymns into his parish.[19]

Charles Wesley carried on the reformation of
hymnwriting begun by Watts and introduced two
new kinds of hymns: the evangelistic hymn and the
hymn of Christian experience. While Watts's hymns
tended to be objective, Wesley incorporated the subjective.[20] In all, Wesley wrote an astonishing six
thousand hymns, including "Hark! The Herald
Angels Sing," "Jesus, Lover of My Soul," and
"Love Divine, All Loves Excelling."

While Watts used the traditional psalm tunes to
accompany his popular poetry, Wesley adopted
new melodies that drew from both the popular
opera and English folk melodies. His compilation,

Hymns on the Great Festivals and Other Occasions, contained twenty-four tunes by a German composer of comic opera.[21] Additionally, he combined folk styles and actual folk tunes with religious texts to form his hymns.[22] His use of Handel's melodies provoked the charge of "worldliness," yet Wesley had no qualms about combining the sacred and secular when it came to the tunes that would carry the biblical message. "It was Wesley's practice to seize upon any song of the theater or the street the moment it became popular and make it carry some newly written hymn into the homes of the people."[23] The tune to "Hark! The Herald Angels Sing" was written by Mendelssohn not to worship God but in praise of the printing press![24]

Worship once again was in a text and tune that the common person could appreciate, and the impact was impressive. The Wesleys gave a high place to hymns in their evangelistic campaigns, and their music had clear lyrics and appealing tunes. Far more than merely a warm-up to the preaching, the hymns were deemed invaluable for the Wesleys' purposes. The majority of the common people were illiterate, but after singing the Wesleys' songs a few times, the message of the gospel and Christian teaching were indelibly imprinted on their minds and hearts.[25]

The Methodist hymns "became the most powerful tool of evangelism England ever knew."[26] The hymns proclaimed the gospel, taught central doctrine of the faith, and provided once again an appealing way for the common person to worship God. As Arnold A. Dallimore put it in his book *A Heart Set Free,*

> *Many a man, many a woman, and many a child went from the meeting, not only deeply affected by the truth heard in the preaching, but also singing over in mind some phrase or even an entire stanza picked up from one of the hymns. When the hymn was heard at a subsequent meeting something more of it was lodged in the memory, it was repeated as the days went by, and, little by little, the entire hymn was learned by heart.[27]*

THE GOSPEL SONG

Gospel songs, such as "Rescue the Perishing" and "The Sweet By and By," are especially associated with the evangelistic songs of the revivals led by Moody and Sankey, beginning in the 1870s, but this style had antecedents in the American folk hymns and camp meeting songs. In America, churches originally sang psalms to slow, monotonous tunes; lively music was thought to be the devil's music.[28] However, when the fires of revival began to spread through the preaching of Jonathan Edwards and George Whitefield, a new song was in order.

The Great Awakening began in 1734 in Northampton, Massachusetts, largely under the preaching of Jonathan Edwards. This revival swept through the American colonies between about 1740 and 1745. Although he personally preferred singing the Psalms, he eventually turned to the hymns of Watts because of the preference of the people. These new hymns had such an impact on the masses that they were sung outside the meetings on the streets and the ferryboats.[29]

Charles Finney (1792–1875) sought to reach the urban masses, the common but educated people in the city. For his purposes, the hymnal's music was too high a standard, while the camp meeting songbook was too low. Responding to this need, Joshua Leavitt compiled *The Christian Lyre* in 1831. His tunes were gleaned from popular songs or were original compositions in the popular style. In the preface he stated: "Every person conversant with revivals must have observed that wherever meetings for prayer and conference assume a special interest, there is a desire to use hymns and music of a different character from those ordinarily used in church."[30]

These new hymns functioned well for the urban masses, but the people of the frontier desired a more lively style of singing. Thus they added their own familiar tunes to the texts of Wesley and Watts. Many of the tunes they used have been traced to "English secular ballads, fiddle tunes (tunes with dance rhythms), marches, and hornpipe tunes."[31]

Rural Baptists in the eighteenth century were

especially apt to express their faith to the tune of popular melodies. Thus, the first Baptist hymnbook, published in 1766, contained many of these tunes. Although labeled "crude" by the more sophisticated, these songs functioned well in the frontier setting.

By the camp meetings of the Second Great Awakening, a period of intense revivalism in America between about 1795 and 1830, some stylistic changes were in order. In the early camp meetings, the texts of Watts, Wesley, Cowper (1731–1800, English hymnwriter who was recognized as the greatest poet of his day whose hymns include "There is a Fountain Filled with Blood"), and Newton (1725–1807, the converted slave trader who became a preacher and wrote hundreds of hymns, among them "Amazing Grace") were sung to tunes that were then popular, but these were not upbeat enough for the new generation. They wanted music that would set their hands to clapping, their feet to tapping, and their bodies to swaying. So they simplified the texts to fit the form of the popular ballad. One such form was to have a verse followed by a chorus where all would join in. Examples of this new form included "I'm Bound for the Promised Land," "Power in the Blood," "When the Roll Is Called Up Yonder," and "Faith Is the Victory."[32] These developments in music, which also were influenced by the Negro spirituals,[33] set the stage for the flowering of the gospel song in the revivals led by Moody and Sankey.

IRA SANKEY

D. L. Moody has been called the greatest evangelist of the nineteenth century. For a period of four months in London in 1875 he held over 285 meetings, with an estimated two million attending.[34] At his meetings in Scotland, halls were filled to capacity with listeners, and hundreds were unable to enter. The results were even more impressive than the attendance. According to Scottish pastor Horatius Bonar, "There was scarcely a Christian household in all Edinburgh in which there were not one or more persons converted during this revival."[35] Were these phenomenal results attributed solely to the anointed preaching? Not according to Moody. He believed that the singing played a crucial role. In his own words,

If you have singing that reaches the heart, it will fill the church every time. . . . Music and song have not only accompanied all scriptural revivals, but are essential in deepening the spiritual life. Singing does at least as much as preaching to impress the Word of God upon people's minds. Ever since God first called me, the importance of praise expressed in song has grown upon me.[36]

In seeking to use music in his campaigns, Moody felt that something new was needed. In his estimation, the camp meeting songs would not be appropriate for the big city masses. Upon hearing the song leading of Ira Sankey in 1870, Moody knew he had found the man and the style.[37]

Trained musicians did not esteem Sankey as an accomplished singer,[38] but he never claimed to be one. He was not seeking to impress serious musicians, but rather to reach the masses with the gospel. His voice and manner had the ability to stir hearts, draw people's attention to the words, and plant a melody within the listener.

As one Edinburgh woman wrote, "Mr. Sankey sings with the conviction that souls are receiving Jesus between one note and the next."[39] His style of song could be described as a popular folk hymnody. A Glasgow journalist described it this way:

> *Much of it is so Scottish and Irish in its construction, that to our people, familiar with such music, it is sometimes difficult to realize that what we hear is sacred song. . . . Is it not possible that this may be why these simple songs have found such a direct and wonderful entrance to the Scottish heart?*[40]

Many people would be repulsed at the notion of clothing sacred songs in a style that was indistinguishable from that of popular tunes, but Moody and Sankey found that this enhanced their ministry. An article by a contemporary of Sankey expressed the approach this way in the *North British Daily Mail:* "He has enriched evangelistic work by something approaching the discovery of a new power.

He spoils the Egyptians of their finest music, and consecrates it to the service of the tabernacle."[41]

Many of the songs were compiled in the hymn-book *Gospel Hymns and Sacred Songs,* published in 1875.[42] Its success in distribution was unprecedented; only the English Bible surpassed it in sales.[43] Together, *Sacred Songs and Solos* and the American version, *Gospel Songs,* were reported to have sold from fifty to eighty million copies in the first fifty years.[44] Although again much chaff was produced with the wheat,[45] many of the songs used in the meetings have survived the winnowing of time, including "Thou Didst Leave Thy Throne," "The Sweet By and By," "Sweet Hour of Prayer," and "Rescue the Perishing."

Not everyone shared this enthusiasm with the novel hymnody. When Moody and Sankey first set foot in Scotland, the people were still devoted to the exclusive use of the Psalms. Horatius Bonar had penned hymns of such enduring quality that they grace the pages of hymnbooks to this day, but in his own day they were banned by the elders of his own parish. The Scots also considered the organ music of Bach and Handel unfit for anything but secular entertainment.[46] As Reverend Henry Davenport Northrop wrote in 1899, "The introduction of hymns into Scottish worship was fought, tooth and nail, as if they were productions of the devil and would overthrow all evangelical religion."[47]

An elderly deacon in Edinburgh expressed the sentiment of much of Scotland when he said to Dr.

Bonar concerning Sankey, "What that one does is an abomination to the Most High! . . . In the first place, he sings hardly any Psalms at all. The ones he does sing are incorrect translations. I won't call it music at all. What he brings to the sanctuary suggests performances in places less religious than churches and chapels."[48]

Sankey accompanied himself with a small reed organ, which with his critics fared no better than his songs. The same elderly deacon referred to it as "a devilish pump machine that wheezes out blasphemously."[49] Another spoke of the organs as having "a devil in every pipe." After Sankey sang "What Shall the Harvest Be?" someone critically remarked to Moody that if he kept singing songs like that, he "would soon have them all dancing."[50]

In the end, though, Sankey's gospel music provided a powerful impetus to the incredible revival that took hold of these lands. And the songs have continued to leave their mark wherever they have been sung.

WILLIAM BOOTH AND THE SALVATION ARMY

While the camp meeting songs functioned well on the American frontier and Sankey's gospel tunes appealed to many in both Europe and America, William Booth (1829–1912) had a burden to reach the common people of England who were not being touched by the traditional church. He resigned his position as a Methodist minister in

1865 to begin a work among the poor in London.
The work became known as the Salvation Army
and eventually spread to more than eighty-six countries. His use of instruments began in the late 1870s
when two members of a brass band were converted. One assisted in leading songs with his cor-
net, and the singing was noticeably improved.[51]
Thus began the use of a vast array of instruments,
including violins, bass viols, *concertives,* brass
instruments, drums, "and anything else that would
make a pleasant sound before the Lord."[52] Interestingly enough, the only instruments not allowed by
Booth were harmoniums, because of their association with chapels and the consequent lack of appeal
to the masses.[53]

The Salvationists brought their instruments
together to form "Hallelujah Bands" and saw multitudes saved who might never have been touched by
the traditional church. Why did these bands have
such an appeal? The secret lay in the Salvationists'
sensitivity to the people they were targeting. The
working men in the industrial communities of
England had experienced a large degree of alien-
ation from the church, but one area that was of
keen interest to them was the secular brass band
movement.[54] Booth's Salvationists found common
ground, putting together their own bands to attract
crowds and proclaim the gospel.

Although Booth himself preferred old Methodist
tunes or an occasional Anglican tune, he found that
many of his unchurched audiences could not sing

them, either because they didn't know the tunes or because they couldn't read. So he took catchy tunes from the music halls[55] and saw the masses respond. Thousands were saved and became Salvationists as a result of listening to the bands.[56] The music was so central to the movement that biographer Bernard Watson wrote, "One way to disarm the Salvation Army would be to take away its music. Without its song . . . the army would be paralyzed."[57]

The tunes used were secular. The tune to "Champaigne Charlie" was sung with "Bless His Name, He Sets Me Free"; "Pretty Louise" became "Living Beneath the Shade of the Cross"; "I Traced Her Little Footsteps in the Snow" became "O, the Blood of Jesus Cleanses White as Snow";[58] "Minnie, Darling, Come and Wander," became "Blessed Savior, Now Behold Me."[59] Some, such as "I've Found a Friend in Jesus" and "He's the Lily of the Valley" (to the tune of "The Old Log Cabin in the Lane"), have endured till the present.

Booth wanted the songs to be simple and in the language of the people—songs that would stick with those who heard them and be hummed as the people went about their daily activities.[60] The resultant style was reported in the *Midland Free Press* as hymns "to tunes that go with a swing and a bang—with a chorus that will force one to sing—and they did seem to strike a tender chord in many a breast that might never have vibrated to any other touch."[61]

But not all viewed these innovations with such sympathy. Victorian clergymen, the press, and local councils showed shocked distaste. Even some of Booth's supporters suggested that the music was irrelevant and superfluous.[62] Others objected that the familiar tunes would remind people of their sinful days. In the long run, though, they found that the new words took prominence and overcame the past sinful associations.[63]

A lesser man would have given in to the taunts of his many critics. But William Booth cared not for the praise of men. His burden was to reach the throngs of lost humanity, and he saw no good reason to dismiss such a useful tool as popular music. As Booth himself put it,

> *Of the soul and citadel of music he [the devil] has taken possession . . . and with it he charms and chains and sways the world. But if sensual, worldly, satanic music wields such a power, what might music not do when songs and hearts and voices were inspired and directed by the Holy Ghost?*[64]

Again, in the Salvation Army publication *The War Cry*, Booth charged his soldiers:

> *Music has a divine effect upon divinely influenced and directed souls. Music is to the soul what wind is to the ship, blowing her onwards in the direction in which she is steered. . . . Not*

*allowed to sing that tune or this tune? Indeed!
Secular music, do you say? Belongs to the
devil does it? Well, if it did, I would plunder
him of it, for he has no right to a single note of
the whole gamut. He's a thief! . . . Every note
and every strain and every harmony is divine,
and belongs to us. . . . So now and for all time
consecrate your voices and your instruments.
Bring out your harps and organs and flutes
and violins and pianos and drums and everything else that can make melody! Offer them
to God and use them to make all hearts about
you merry before the Lord!*[65]

11

What we can Learn From History

What experience and history teach is this—that peoples and governments never have learned anything from history, or acted on principles deduced from it.

Hegel[1]

The styles of song tunes and lyrics were not the only aspects of church music that changed, and thus evoked consternation, throughout the years. In this chapter we will consider further innovations, attempting to glean insights from history that will shed light on the present controversy.

THE ORGAN

The organ as we know it has been traced to the hydraulis or water organ of the third century B.C., possibly invented by Ktesibius, an Alexandrian engineer. It became popular and accompanied outdoor events such as circuses and gladiator combats.[2] This early organ may even have accompanied the slaughter of early Christians in the Roman arena![3] Not until the thirteenth century was the organ incorporated into the Mass,[4] but even then it was not without its opponents.[5]

By the time of the Reformation the organ was quite at home in the Catholic church. Yet the association of instruments with Catholicism gave it a bad reputation among some of the reformers, who promptly condemned its use.[6]

The magistrates in Zurich decreed in 1524 that there should be "no more playing of organs in the city and in the churches."[7] Soon thereafter, the organ of the Great Minster was broken into pieces. Calvin shunned the instrument, and through his great influence, many organs were destroyed in succeeding years.[8] This instrument's banishment was so complete among certain groups that by 1727 only one organ could be found in all the churches of Scotland. Its return from exile would not come soon or easily.

To the Scots, the organ became known as the "Kist O' Whistles"; to the English it was "the devil's bagpipe." Authorization to use organs in the Presbyterian church did not come about until the Established church granted permission in 1866, followed by the United Presbyterian church in 1872.[9]

In the New World, the early Puritans would have been horrified at the thought of an organ in their church. Over the years the question of organs became a serious issue, on occasion erupting into bitter controversy. The eminent Cotton Mather (1663–1728, pastor of Boston's North Church and prolific writer) argued that if organs were permitted, other instruments would later be acceptable, and then dancing would follow![10]

Eventually many churches surrendered to the organ, but sometimes only after a battle. The first non-Episcopal church to acquire an organ was the Congregational church at Providence in 1770. The Brattle Street Church in Boston finally consented to order an organ from England. However, after the organ was ordered the congregation lapsed into a bitter, divisive controversy (see chapter 9). Many people of the Brattle Street Church were shocked and horrified that such a great evil was being welcomed into the church by members who claimed to love God more than the world.[11]

OTHER INNOVATIONS

Church musicians of the Middle Ages believed the augmented fourth chord to be possessed by the devil,[12] yet since that time this chord has been used extensively in the church.[13] At another time, thirds and sixths were considered sensual, and thus banned.[14] Later the syncopated beat was rejected because of its associations with the ragtime era, but hymns like "Since Jesus Came into My Heart" survived the initial shock of many skeptical worshipers and today are considered traditional hymns.[15]

The piano seems rather harmless to the church member of the 1990s, but few nineteenth-century churches would have considered using such a secular instrument![16] Eighteenth-century Moravians accepted many instruments, but rejected the violin since it was associated with the dance and was labeled "the devil's fiddle."[17]

During the liturgical movement (c. 1930–1960), when churches took a new interest in historic forms and practices of worship, the corporate experience was glorified and the solo shunned as too personal, something that glorified the singer.[18] Early "Free Churches," which broke from the state churches in Europe, vehemently opposed the choir as "popish" because of associations with the Roman Church.[19]

Sadly, the very tools God has given us to joyfully use in edifying one another and glorifying him have often become battlefields throughout church history. Many of these battles seem senseless or even comical in retrospect, but at the time they were serious and divisive.

It is my hope that the following reflections on the historical data will prove valuable in helping us to better understand and respond to the present controversy.

REFLECTIONS: THE PAST SPEAKS

1. *Each period of musical transition follows a cyclical pattern.*[20] The first stage, which we will call *Separation*, finds old forms of music firmly entrenched in the church. These styles communicate almost exclusively to those who have grown up in the church, alienating the uninitiated. The musical style of the church is separated from popular styles understood by the common folk, the former being labeled sacred, the latter secular. What was once

effective salt has lost its savor, and the stage is set for Phase 2: *Integration.*

Bold innovators, convinced that outdated forms are stifling heartfelt worship, adopt the musical language (often the actual tunes) of the common person, much to the chagrin of diehard traditionalists. The guardians of the past counter, ushering in Phase 3: *Conflict.*

At this point, the innovations are bitterly denounced as compromise with the world, subbiblical, use of the devil's music, replacement of good worship with cheap entertainment, and a host of other concerns. Enter Phase 4: *Renewal.*

Although renewal isn't brought about entirely by the musical shift, it certainly is enhanced greatly by the communicative power of the new medium. Worship again is in the language of the people, and church music becomes an integral part of the believers' everyday lives as they carry their heartfelt songs outside the church walls into the factory and the marketplace.

Finally, what was once new and fresh becomes standard. What was once condemned as secular finds its way into the hymnbook and is considered sacred. At the same time, the popular style of the common person has continued to change so that there is once again a dichotomy between the traditional and the popular. What once bred excitement now elicits yawns. Even so, no one would dream of adopting popular "worldly" forms. And so we find ourselves back at Phase 1, and history repeats itself.

Since it would seem that the contemporary Christian music of today is following the same historical pattern, wisdom dictates that we take great pains to avoid the errors that have consistently accompanied each stage.

2. *A style's dubious origins or bad associations don't preclude God's ability to use it for his purposes.* History has shown that the use of styles originated in and popularized by the world has been abundantly successful in the church. God can use—and has used—many popular styles to further his message. So the historical perspective demonstrates that the current issue shouldn't be whether or not to use the styles of "the world." Both traditional and contemporary church styles were, at one time, developed, popularized, and used by the world. Thus, the question, Should we incorporate the styles of the world into the church? becomes moot in the light of history. The only question we must resolve is, Which era of the world's music will we use?

3. *Subjective convictions on musical style cannot always be trusted.* If we agree that the musical styles adopted by Luther and Sankey and the poetic style adopted by Watts were all legitimate, then we must conclude that many of their contemporaries were misguided in their conviction that these styles were evil.

Perhaps critics had mistakenly associated the church music of their upbringing with God's style and the popular forms with the devil's style. When

the seemingly sacred and seemingly profane were
finally wed, the new church forms still reeked of
worldliness, ingrained cultural rules were broken,
and many saints called a foul. Today those on both
sides of the controversy would agree that many
saints of the past erred in prematurely condemning
what was later judged, by common consensus of
the church, to be some of our greatest hymnody.
Apparently, for those who objected, the inner voice
of their cultural heritage was crying out and was
mistaken for the voice of the Spirit. Is it really so
difficult to imagine that the same tragic error is
being perpetuated in our own time?

Theologian J. I. Packer played jazz at the age of
eighteen but laid it aside at his conversion, assuming that its pursuit could never be reconciled with
total surrender to Christ. He could not see, in his
own words, "how this or any other form of secular
music or art could be pursued with a Christian
motivation." His associates felt that the music "had
a devilish influence on its devotees." Later in life
Packer began to question his early assumptions and
concluded that "early jazz was among the twentieth century's most valuable cultural products."[21]
Today the music he once shunned is a source of joy
and refreshment to him.

The path of Packer's musical pilgrimage has been
followed by many others in regard to the rock style
of music. In the light of these contemporary and historical examples, negative first impressions must be
subjected to rigorous, critical scrutiny before they

are prematurely assumed to be the promptings of the Spirit.

4. *Those who strive to avoid all controversy may find themselves on the periphery of God's move.* According to church music historian Millar Patrick, "All great spiritual movements are cradled in controversy."[22] If this is true, we cannot afford the luxury of an unstudied neutrality.

Music has been a central factor in the ushering in of renewal throughout church history. According to church music historian W. C. Proctor, "Hymns and spiritual songs have always accompanied times of spiritual revival."[23] Donald Hustad notes that "the history of revivalism has seen a repeated flowering of new sacred music forms which sprang from secular roots." Hustad goes on to note the reason for its power: "Musical sounds common to the secular world are effective in 'preevangelizing' the uncommitted."[24] However, the very factor that makes this music effective among the uncommitted makes it controversial among those in the church. To ignore the controversy and cling to methods that worked for past generations could mean, at best, missing the renewing winds of the Spirit. At worst, it could mean resisting the hand of God.

5. *Tradition drives in stakes that are difficult to remove.* Peter Lord, pastor of Park Avenue Baptist Church in Titusville, Florida, has observed that those most resistant to the present move of God are often those who were a part of the last move of God. Rather than being open to new methods and

forms, we assume that the way to revival in the present is to recreate the way it occurred in the past. In two of the meetings led by Moody and Sankey in Scotland, a lady cried out as she made her way to the door, "Let me 'oot! Let me 'oot! What would John Knox think of the like of you?"[25]

Apparently, she knew something of the work of God through John Knox, but her bondage to that tradition would not allow her to see God's hand in a new work. Traditions can be beneficial, but we must constantly evaluate them as to their biblical base and their ability to function in a new generation.

Keep in mind the lessons of history as we approach the contemporary scene and consider how to harness the powerful medium of music in our own generation.

PART FOUR

HARNESSING THE POWER OF CONTEMPORARY MUSIC

12

THE NEED FOR AN ALTERNATIVE

*Behold, I send you out as sheep in the midst of
wolves; therefore be shrewd as serpents, and innocent as doves.*

Matthew 10:16

Toto, I don't think we're in Kansas anymore.
Dorothy in *The Wizard of Oz*

Allan Bloom of the University of Chicago, in his far-
reaching critique of American higher education,
The Closing of the American Mind, devoted an
entire chapter to an analysis of the present state of
music. As to its centrality to our culture, Bloom
stated, "Nothing is more singular about this generation than its addiction to music. Today, a large proportion of young people between the ages of ten
and twenty live for music. It is their passion. Nothing else excites them as it does. They cannot take
seriously anything alien to music. When they are in
school and with their families, they are longing to
plug themselves back into their music."[1]

Bloom is right on target. An estimated three hundred thousand professional and amateur rock groups are performing in the United States alone,[2] and they are not hard-pressed for an audience. A recent study by the American Medical Association noted that the average teen listens to 10,500 hours of rock music (more than twice the time they will spend in class at school) on their journey from the seventh to the twelfth grades and concluded that music exerts a greater influence on teens than even television.[3]

In response, most youth affirm that they enjoy the music but deny that they listen to the lyrics. Yet Bob Demoss, founder and director of Teen Vision, routinely distributes tests when he speaks at schools and has found that even young children have memorized the words to popular songs. When fourth-graders were asked to complete this line from a popular Samantha Fox song "Touch Me (I Want Your_____)," 80 percent correctly identified the missing word: "Body."[4] Fourth graders.

Music stars are more than mere creators of background music to our kids; they are heroes. A survey by the *World Almanac and Book of Facts* asked four thousand high school students to name their heroes. Among the top eight were Debbie Allen (of the rock-laden television show, *Fame*), Bruce Springsteen, Madonna, Prince, and Eddie VanHalen.[5]

Like it or not, music is a major component of most teens' lives. It impacts their decisions and provides their heroes. Parents, ministers, and all who work with youth should know what these groups stand for and what they are communicating. That's why it is so amazing that most adults are rather oblivious to the whole music scene. For those who have been on the periphery of the popular music phenomenon, the following pages will provide a shocking primer to the field.

The apostle Paul stated that he was not unaware of the devil's schemes (2 Cor. 2:11), yet many parents have assumed that Junior was safe in his room, off the devil's streets, when actually the evil one was quite at home in Junior's bedroom, gaining safe access through his earphones.

If the following information seems shocking beyond belief, simply check the compact disc graphics at your local music store or browse through music magazines at the supermarket. Some of the most shocking examples have been left out because of their inappropriateness in print. And, no, these are not obscure, underground bands. These are some of the most popular bands in tape sales over the years.

CULT AND OCCULT INVOLVEMENT

For those nations, which you shall dispossess, listen to those who practice witchcraft and to diviners, but as for you, the Lord your God has not allowed you to do so. (Deut. 18:14)

Tina Turner is one of the longest-running hit

rock stars ever to record a song. By the time of a
March 4, 1985, *Newsweek* report, her *Private
Dancer* record had gone triple platinum (3 million
copies). But what about her personal convictions?
She believes in reincarnation (contrary to Heb.
9:27), and purports to have once lived in ancient
Egypt and *belle epoque* France.[6]

For many rock artists, their occult beliefs are not
hidden in the closet but are shouted from the house-
tops. As bizzare as it may seem, occult themes
make for good advertising in the music business,
and the stage has often been transformed into a pulpit for these preachers of apostasy.

In 1976, *Newsweek* revealed folk singer John
Denver as "a self-appointed messiah" who "view[s]
his music as far more than just entertainment. He
sees it as . . . the gospel of a new secular religion
whose godhead is one's own head."[7] According to
Denver, "One of these days I'll be so complete I
won't be human. I'll be a god."[8] Led Zeppelin was
at one time crowned the most popular band in the
world, with their song "Stairway to Heaven" proclaimed the best song of the seventies. Jimmy Page,
guitarist for Led Zeppelin, was so absorbed in the
occult that he purchased his own occult bookstore.
Hit Parader magazine quoted him as saying,
"There was not one good collection of books on
the occult in London, and I was tired of having to
go to different places to get the books I wanted."
Page was so immersed in the occult that he bought
Boleskine, the former mansion in Scotland of Aleis-

ter Crowley, who was one of the most famous occult figures of our age.[9] Black Sabbath's album *Sabbath, Bloody Sabbath* features a nude satanic ritual on the cover complete with the number 666, the mark of the beast according to Revelation 13:18.

SEX

> *Do not be deceived; neither fornicators, nor idolators, nor adulterers, nor effeminate, nor homosexuals . . . shall inherit the kingdom of God. (1 Cor. 6:9)*

God's Word restricts sex to the marriage relationship, but much of contemporary music preaches free sex, even to the point of extolling deviant forms. One study examined 166 concept videos and found over 75 percent to contain visual presentations of sexual intimacy.[10] In a study of country music in 1986, sociologist Edward G. Armstrong concluded that "the primary topic of country songs is love, especially cheatin' love."[11] Voyeurism and autoeroticism are combined in the country songs "It's Me Again, Margaret" and "Plastic Girl."[12]

In the pop scene, Whitney Houston's hit song "Saving All My Love for You" expresses the desire of a woman to have sex with a married man. The Bible calls this adultery. The style is a mellow sound that appeals to most adults.[13]

Turning to rock, Prince has attracted a sizable following and was proclaimed Artist of the Year by *Rolling Stone* magazine in 1982. His third album, *Dirty Mind,* sported X-rated lyrics and featured Prince himself on the album cover, dressed in a trench coat and black bikini. This cover harmonizes well with the philosophy of life Prince espouses: "I guess if there's a concept, it's freedom—personal freedom—and the fact that we all have to do what we want to do."[14]

Guns 'n Roses was one of the most popular groups in 1988. Sexual violence is featured both on their debut album cover and in the album's lyrics.[15] Simon le Bon of Duran Duran said of sex: "It's always been an important part of Duran's songs. It's always been the most important thing on my mind."[16]

Bronski Beat emerged as "nearly every Englishman's choice for the best band of 1984," according to *Rolling Stone* magazine. The band was composed of three men in their early twenties who were openly gay and wrote songs about their life-style. Their first album? "The Age of Consent."[17]

W.A.S.P. has been known to throw raw meat to their audiences and drink blood from a skull. Additionally, one stage show found them simulating a ritual torture of a scantily clad woman tied to a rack.[18] Stephen Pearcy, lead singer for Ratt, stated, "My whole concept of women and touring is that it's like eating. You'd get tired of the same meal every day, so it wouldn't be worth anyone's while to be confined to just one."[19]

DRUGS

And do not get drunk with wine, for that is dissipation. (Eph. 5:18)

The Bible denounces drunkenness and, by implication, the recreational use of drugs, but drugs are promoted by many groups who brag of their drunken revelries and sing of their experiences. "License to Ill," the best-selling album by The Beastie Boys, refers to drugs and alcohol over ninety times.[20]

Grace Slick of Jefferson Starship stated, "Handfuls of rock groups have been liberated by the use of LSD. We all use drugs and condone the use of drugs for everyone."[21]

VIOLENCE AND REBELLION

Therefore he who resists authority has opposed the ordinance of God; and they who have opposed will receive condemnation upon themselves. (Rom. 13:2)

The National Coalition on Television Violence has reported violence in over half of all MTV videos.[22] A 1984 study found "eighteen instances of aggression each hour on Music Television (MTV),

35 percent of which depict sexual violence against women."[23]

Jim Morrison of The Doors, commenting on his stage performances, stated, "I'm god up there! I do what I want! I'm interested in anything about revolution, disorder, chaos, sex, and especially activity that has no meaning."[24]

HYPE VERSUS AGENDA

But isn't it all just hype? Has our generation just devolved to such a low state of religion that what would have warranted burning at the stake in earlier generations is today a successful marketing gimmick?

Granted, for some all the sex talk and rebellion is probably just hype. For instance, one group with a wild reputation is AC/DC, but in an interview with *Hit Parader* one of the members was asked, "What makes touring so fun for AC/DC?" The response?

> *I'm not saying that we're one of those bands that break up hotel rooms and hang out with hundreds of ladies. We're all family men, and we're too old for that kind of stuff anyway. But when you're on tour you can concentrate on what you enjoy doing most, and not have to worry about things like mowing the lawn or making sure there's enough gas in the car.*[25]

Motley Crue uses a pentagram, a symbol used in satanism, on their albums, but are the members really satanic? "The pentagram is not necessarily demonic," says Nikki Sixx of the Crue. "I've done some research into ancient symbolism, and the pentagram was an ancient symbol of evil. There's nothing about the devil associated with it. If certain cults have picked up on the pentagram, that's their business. It's of no interest to me."[26]

Breathing a sigh of relief? Hardly. The present association of the pentagram with satanism may be of no interest to Nikki Sixx, but it *is* of interest to youth who are introduced to the occult through bands like Motley Crue. Kids want to be like their heroes, and many imitate what they believe is the religion of their heroes. To give a wild concert admonishing fans to rebel against authority, pursue free sex, and ingest drugs, and then to follow it with a newspaper review stating that the band members are just family men putting on a show to pay the mortgage is on a par with the Pied Piper leading the children into oblivion and then proclaiming, "Just kidding!"

But for some groups, an agenda motivates their music—an agenda that has nothing to do with media hype or record sales. Their music is propaganda for a cause.

The late Jimi Hendrix, still a guitar idol for many aspiring musicians, once stated, "I can explain everything better through music. You hypnotize people to where they go right back to their natural state, and when you get people at their weakest point, you can preach into their subconscious what we want to say."[27]

"Pop music is a popular method of conditioning the way people think!" says Graham Nash of Crosby, Stills, and Nash. "I figured the only thing to do was to swipe their kids. By saying that, I'm not talking about kidnapping; I'm talking about changing their value systems, which removes them from their parents' world very effectively."[28]

Jacques Morali of The Village People stated, "I formed this group as a personal protest against Anita Bryant and to make gays more acceptable in our society."[29]

Said a member of Jefferson Starship: "Our music is intended to broaden the generation gap [and] to alienate children from their parents."[30]

The Enemy is no longer restricted to subtle schemes and cold war tactics. The principalities and powers have left the trenches and exposed themselves with unparalleled clarity—and many of our citizens are delighted to pay $30 to watch the show.

13

COMMUNICATING MUSICAL CONVICTIONS TO YOUR CHILDREN

To act without clear understanding, to form habits without investigation, to follow a path all one's life without knowing where it really leads—such is the behavior of the multitude.

Menclus

And, fathers, do not provoke your children to anger; but bring them up in the discipline and instruction of the Lord.

Ephesians 6:4

Most Christian adults are filled with righteous indignation at this point and may be gathering wood even now for a tape burning—but not so fast. Our object is to rid our family and friends of the evil influence of certain artists, and record burnings have not always proven successful in this regard.[1]

The destruction of a seventeen-year-old's tapes against his will may only drive a wedge between parent and child and inadvertently enhance the lure of rebellious music whenever the parents are

161

absent. Remember, we have been called to shape our children's values without exasperating them. The approach must be given much thought and prayer, tailoring the strategy to the individual situation.

The concerned parent should read Al Menconi's *Today's Music: A Window to Your Child's Soul.* Some of the following principles of confrontation were gleaned from his insightful book.

1. *Work on your relationship with the child.* If a parent has failed to spend quality time with a child, walls of resentment may have built up that must be torn down before lasting values can be communicated. If a daughter has taken refuge in a rock subculture because of the absence or neglect of her parents, don't be surprised if she clings tenaciously to her music.

As trivial as the posters, concerts, tapes, and T-shirts may appear to the casual observer, these trinkets have become by default the very foundation that supports the world of many teenagers. Their musical world brings them relief from their emotional struggles and communicates with them when they are lonely. They cannot imagine life apart from their music any more than many upper-middle-class adults could imagine life apart from their country club membership.

Consequently, the parental S.W.A.T. team that converges on an unsuspecting son, ransacking his bedroom in an effort to purify his home, may win the battle but lose the child. In the long run, the alienated son will probably find a way to reclaim his musical world, only this time with a vengeance.

Al Menconi asks a penetrating question in this regard: "Today's rock musicians communicate their values to your child every day. Do you?"[2] If you don't, or if you do not even have the relational foundation from which to communicate values, you urgently need to take steps to get in touch with your child.

2. *If you communicate well, and your child recognizes that whatever you say comes only from your love, take the next step of self-examination.* Jesus said that before I can even consider taking a speck out of my brother's eye, I should take the beam out of my own eye. In other words, if you preach an anti-rock message to your children, supporting your thesis with evidence that listening habits affect our behavior, then don't hop into your car and relax to the beer-guzzling country tunes of Hank Williams, Jr. And don't denounce the sex and violence of MTV if the videos you rent portray the same life-style. Teenagers can smell hypocrisy a mile away, and although they may acquiesce to your standards in your presence, they will adopt your life-style in your absence.

3. *Gain an understanding of your child's musical world.* It is strange that so few parents take an interest in an area that is so important to their children. If a wife immersed herself in the world of art, spending hours each day at the canvas and delighting in the works of the masters, she probably

would take offense if her husband totally ignored this vital area of her life. Yet many parents show complete disinterest in the music for which their children practically live.

Your teens may listen to none of the aforementioned groups, but do you know what groups they do listen to? Is there anything positive about the group's musicianship or message that you could appreciate with your child? If you wish to guarantee a closed ear, then dogmatically denounce the musical style as not even worthy to be called music, the musicianship as a joke, and the entire enterprise as a bunch of hoodlums in silly costumes banging drums and screaming at the top of their lungs. Such comments only reinforce your child's feelings that you have no understanding of his or her world.

Remember, kids may flunk math, but they are experts on their music. They know that Sting (of The Police) formerly taught in a Catholic school—not exactly your stereotypic hoodlum—and most teens can tell a talented guitarist from a hacker. Eddie VanHalen is an excellent rock guitarist. Many of these musicians have completed formal music training and are outstanding musicians. So communicate understanding by noting that the drummer for Rush is outstanding. After the child recovers from the initial shock of your compliment, you may be in a better position to express concerns over life-styles and lyrics. Take an interest in your children's world, and they may take an interest in yours.

4. *Seek to build convictions, not mere compliance.* A thorough education regarding biblical standards of music cannot be gained in a thirty-minute talk. Instructional videos and books may need to be studied as a family. The following biblical principles could be profitably discussed to provide a rationale for choosing positive music.

1. God is concerned with the renewing of our minds, not just our actions (see Rom. 12:1-2). Long after a tape has been ejected, the songs continue to play in our minds. Our minds are like computers, our current thoughts determined by our past input. Songs play over and over in our mind. At the very least, they have an impact on the contents of our thoughts, the subjects of our meditation.

God gives us specific guidelines as to the proper objects of meditation. Christian minds should dwell on things that are true, pure, right, lovely, honorable, and worthy of praise (see Phil. 4:8). The blessed man meditates on God's law day and night (Ps. 1:2). Can we apply these clear injunctions while ingesting a steady diet of AC/DC, Black Sabbath, and Judas Priest? Obviously not. Believers set themselves up for frustrated, defeated lives when they determine with their wills to live a pure life but program their minds with lust and violence.

2. Music can affect life-styles. Although it would be difficult to design a study to conclusively prove that negative songs cause negative behavior over the long haul, there are studies that at least support this thesis. An Illinois State University study con-

cluded that "certain types of rock videos can foster in men a calloused and antagonistic . . . orientation toward women."[3] According to psychiatrist Robert S. Demski, chief of staff at Laurel Ridge Hospital in San Antonio, "By repeated exposure to cynicism, hatred, and indiscriminate destruction, especially without the balance of parental love and counsel, children become desensitized to brutality and degradation."[4]

Another study found seventh- and tenth-graders "more likely to approve of premarital sex" after watching selected music videos.[5] It would seem reasonable that repeated exposure might produce long-term changes in attitudes and behavior.[6]

3. By listening to ungodly groups, purchasing their tapes, and attending their concerts, we finance causes subversive to our worldview. It is amazing that people who would never send a donation to the Church of Satan think nothing of buying a Black Sabbath album and T-shirt.

4. Each of us influences others by our activities. The apostle Paul wrote, "The things you have learned and received and heard and seen in me, practice these things; and the God of peace shall be with you" (Phil. 4:9). Could you encourage young Christians to practice what they see in your choice of music?

5. The successful gardener must do more than merely love flowers. He must hate weeds. In the same way, the Christian life involves hating evil as well as loving good. Paul admonishes the Romans

to "abhor what is evil" (Rom. 12:9). Another translation puts it this way: "Regard evil with horror."[7] If, therefore, we truly abhor the message a song is conveying, how can we enjoy listening to it?

6. According to Jesus, the greatest commandment is, "You shall love the LORD your God with all your heart, and with all your soul, and with all your mind" (Matt. 22:37). Think of the person you love most here on earth. Further, imagine that a rock group produced an album that mocks this person and ridicules everything for which this person stands. Do you think that you could buy this album and enjoy the music? Your love for the person would naturally produce an abhorrence for the production, even if the tunes would be otherwise appealing. How then can people say that they love God and yet take pleasure in songs that promote and glorify the very things that cause Him such sorrow?

5. *We need to help youth break through the illusion that their music heroes have found peace and fulfillment through success at their vocation.* They must learn to see through the plastic world staged in television studios and concert halls.

Let them know that Sting, super-successful bassist and songwriter for The Police, is not necessarily happy. "What's the most widely held misconception of success?" Sting was asked in an interview. His response? "That it brings you happiness. It doesn't, and I don't think anything does. I have massive success and no friends. I would say I have three very close friends. The public tends to imagine that rock stars have millions of friends. I don't." [8]

John Cougar Mellencamp stated, "When you get older . . . it's hard to be happy. I never had a full day since I was twenty-one."[9]

Lindsay Buckingham of Fleetwood Mac said, "I'm lonely. My personal life is fairly barren. A house [worth $2 million] full of new furniture doesn't mean a whole lot. It just means you have a nice place to watch TV. But so what? I feel pretty isolated at the moment. I'm sort of like a guy on the top of a hill in a little castle of his own. I hope that won't last forever."[10]

On September 17, 1970 rock guitar idol Jimi Hendrix smoked pot, drank wine, swallowed sleeping pills, and then went to bed and choked on his own vomit.[11] When Janis Joplin heard of his death, she cursed and lamented, "He beat me to it." Two weeks later, her syphilis-riddled body was found, her life cut short by an overdose of heroin.[12] Sid Vicious of the Sex Pistols killed his girlfriend and then overdosed on drugs. He was twenty-one; his girlfriend, twenty.[13] Hank Williams, Sr., of country music fame, died in the back seat of a car of a drug overdose and heart failure.[14]

The list could go on and on. James Honeyman-Scott of the Pretenders died of heart failure due to cocaine. Brian Jones of the Rolling Stones drowned as a result of a drug overdose.

Our generation has been fed a lie. Many sincerely believe that one of God's most enjoyable pastimes is searching the world for people having a good time, so that he can ruin it. To the contrary, Jesus came to give us life, and to give it more abundantly (see John 10:10). "No good thing does He withhold from those who walk uprightly" (Ps. 84:11).

In other words, God's negative commands are for a positive purpose. He knows that a life-style of recreational drugs, promiscuous sex, and unbridled parties leads to misery. He's not an Almighty Party Pooper. He just wants to spare his children the misery that the world reaps every day as a direct result of the seeds they have sown.

As parents work with their children and pastors with their flocks, they must communicate the spirit as well as the letter of the law. Only then will our children not only know the truth, but have the motivation to follow it.

14

A Christian Alternative

Do not be overcome by evil, but overcome evil with good.

Romans 12:21

When people resolve to give up their unhealthy music, a significant step has been taken. Unfortunately, without a second step many will regress into their old ways. From Al Menconi's vast experience, when people return to their secular music they are even more devoted to it than before.[1] The problem? They were originally sincere about giving up the old, but they were never given a viable alternative.

In our society, people will not live in a musical vacuum. It is likely that most people would fail in an attempt to revamp their stylistic heritage by restricting themselves to traditional hymns. Some may succeed. Most won't. If we wish to see permanent change in this area, we must suggest viable alternatives in a palatable style.

There are secular groups that sing positive music. Just as a secular artist can paint a wholesome, beautiful picture, so can a secular musician produce beautiful music. Many of the songs on the market today simply expresses emotional love, and there's nothing wrong with falling in love. But in programming our thought lives, committed Christians should consider the incredible potential that Christian music affords for mind transformation. There is nothing wrong with listening to songs about legitimate relationships between girls and guys, but how many people with normal hormones need more motivation to think about that particular topic? I certainly didn't as a teenager. That's why I decided to listen to Christian music, which proved to be a decision that has reaped tremendous rewards through the years. My mind has been filled with God's Word, comforted in times of stress or loss, and challenged when tempted to apathy.

Unfortunately, contemporary Christian music remains a well-kept secret in many circles. A recent study by the Barna Research Group found that only 43 percent of the teens surveyed had heard of Petra, 28 percent of Michael W. Smith, and 15 percent of DeGarmo and Key—three of our most popular groups targeting young people. By way of contrast, a whopping 99 percent had heard of secular artists such as Bon Jovi, Madonna, and New Kids on the Block. When Christian teens were surveyed, only 52 percent had heard of Petra and 20 percent of DeGarmo and Key—but 91 percent had heard of secular groups Ton Loc and L. L. Cool J.[2]

The bottom line is this: 85 percent of kids in church are living on a steady diet of 3.5 hours of secular pop and rock radio every day.[3] The world is winning a key battle in the war for the minds of our youth, and this is happening at the same time that we may be witnessing what Hustad calls "the most significant new development in Christian witness music since Ira Sankey popularized the gospel song more than one hundred years ago!"[4]

Many Christian groups are producing quality music in every style imaginable. As I write, Christians are producing pop, rap, rhythm and blues, traditional, jazz, acappella, country, black contemporary gospel, adult contemporary, soft rock, hard rock, thrash/speed metal, pop/melodic metal, house, rave, and probably any other style enjoyed by those of any age group. Teenagers who are aware of Christian groups playing their styles tend to like them.[5] But regrettably, according to George Barna, the groups are "virtually unknown to the teenage market."[6] It is time that church leaders began to seriously promote this music among congregations that desperately need an alternative.

This chapter will introduce the ministries of a few contemporary Christian artists. They were selected not so much for their popularity, but because I have followed their ministries over the years. Those playing the rock style are spotlighted here, since this is where the controversy most often erupts.

PETRA
When Nikki Sixx of the secular band Motley Crue was asked what would have happened if their band

had not made it into the big time, he replied, "We'd probably all be in jail." What would the members of Petra do in the event of a breakup? When asked, they each replied that they would labor for the Lord in another ministry, finding other ways to communicate the gospel.[7] We hardly need the gift of discernment to choose the best alternative.

Petra is the most popular Christian rock band in the world, but their humble beginnings belied any dreams for success. Founded in 1972 in Indiana, they played wherever they could—in churches, high schools, parks, and prisons, and at retreats. They were breaking new ground, and only a burden to reach young people could keep them ministering through years of obscurity. After producing three albums, none of which fared well financially, only Bob Hartman, founder and lead guitarist, felt they should continue as a band.

Those who accuse these bands of delusions of grandeur and financial gain need to remember the dismal market for a Christian rock band in the early seventies. Sure, the local youth of Fort Wayne loved them, but what Christian bookstore would carry rock, and what Christian radio station would play it? Christian radio shied away from the rock style; secular radio couldn't stomach the Christian lyrics.

Even so, Hartman's burden to minister to the rock generation prevailed, and he regrouped with three musicians whom he met at a Bible study: bassist Mark Kelly, keyboardist John Slick, and drum-

mer Louie Weaver. Greg Volz joined Petra as vocalist, demonstrating his disregard for worldly fame
by turning down an offer to sing for the popular
secular band R.E.O. Speedwagon.

Attendance grew from an average of 764 in their
"Never Say Die" tour (1981) to more than eight
thousand at an "On Fire" concert in 1988.[8] But the
road to success has not been an easy one. Billy Ray
Hearn, president of the Sparrow Corporation and
early producer for Petra, said that in their early years

> *They were probably put down more than any*
> *band I ever heard. But they stayed together.*
> *They hung in there. They had more tenacity*
> *and "stick-to-itiveness" than any group I have*
> *seen. They lived through the hard days and*
> *finally won. My greatest "hat's off" to them*
> *for hanging in through the tough times—and*
> *when they made it, it didn't change them.*
> *They didn't go to the market; the market*
> *finally came to them.[9]*

Again, popularity and musical prowess are not
the bottom line in evaluating a band. When popular Christian speaker and author Josh McDowell
was asked to tour with Petra, he launched a major
research effort to inspect the fruit of both their lives
and their ministry. His conclusion after checking
them out and living with them on tour? "In twenty-
five years of ministry I've worked with people all
over the world, and I've never worked with people

more godly than the guys in Petra."[10] After each concert, Josh "found himself more in love with Jesus and more committed to His Lordship in his life."[11]

What about the fruit of Petra's ministry? During their most recent tour it was not uncommon to see one or two hundred individuals making commitments and talking with counselors at the close of a show. Who can calculate the spiritual growth fostered by those listening to Petra's tapes from day to day?

The group's songs are anything but shallow. "Get on Your Knees and Fight Like a Man" challenges listeners to persevere in prayer. "Chameleon" blasts the lukewarm, hypocritical Christian life so prevalent today. "First Love" depicts the supreme love of the believer for his Savior. Other songs, such as "Creed," bring the forte of Charles Wesley—teaching doctrine through song—into the twentieth century.

"CREED"

I believe in God the Father—maker of heaven
    and earth
And in Jesus Christ His only Son
I believe in the virgin birth
I believe in the Man of Sorrows bruised for
    iniquities,
I believe in the Lamb who was crucified and
    hung between two thieves

I believe in the resurrection on that third and
    glorious day
And I believe in the empty tomb and the stone
    that the angel rolled away
He descended and set the captives free
And now He sits at God's right hand and pre-
    pares a place for me

Chorus:
This is my creed—the witness I have heard
The faith that has endured
This truth is assured
Through the darkest ages past
Though persecuted it will last
And I will hold steadfast to this creed

I believe He sent His Spirit to comfort and to
    reveal
To lead us into truth and light, to baptize and
    to seal
I believe that He will come back the way He
    went away
And receive us all unto Himself, but no man
    knows the day

Chorus

I believe He is the Judge of all men, small and
    great
The resurrected souls of men receive from Him
    their fate

Some to death and some to life, some to their
    reward
Some to sing eternal praise forever to our Lord

Chorus

Imagine the mind-renewing potential of music
like this saturating the minds of young people day
after day. The style is one they will listen to; the
timeless message is one they need to hear.

This is the bottom line for Bob Hartman: "How
many kids can we reach and how many lives can
we change with what we do? We are missionaries,
and missionaries must learn the language of the
people they are trying to reach."[12]

KEITH GREEN

If there ever was a prophetic voice in contemporary
Christian music, it was Keith Green. Green found
Christ in 1975 after a search through drugs, free
love, money, fame, and "enlightenment" through a
study of the great teachers and philosophers who
have impacted the world. From the time of his conversion he began to develop a zeal for God. Of
those early years he wrote,

> *We would witness at the beach, at the park,
> in restaurants, even to wrong numbers on
> the phone. Then came those who had
> nowhere to stay, no money, no friends. . . .
> Those were crazy days! People sleepin' on*

the couch, in all the rooms, even on the garage floor! Some Christians thought we had gone too far. Well, maybe we did, but God blessed both our boldness and innocence . . . many got saved and many found hope. Sure we got ripped-off, even robbed . . . but each soul was worth it![13]

So began the spiritual life of Keith Green, a man who communicated to many the concepts of holiness and radical commitment. During his life he consistently held up the standard of God's holy Word and abhorred all that hinted of compromise. According to evangelist Leonard Ravenhill, Green

had a holy zeal and a purity I've seen in very few. I don't think Green was preoccupied with the gospel of Christ as much as he was with the person of Christ. I think that was his consuming passion. He wasn't just a preacher. He was a crusader. And he poured out the inner passion of his soul through the vibrant lyrics of his songs.[14]

Although he has now departed to be with the one he so longed to be with, his message continues to make an impact through his tapes, newsletters, tracts, and "Last Days Ministries," led by his wife, Melody.

Green's records contain such songs as "I Pledge

My Head to Heaven," written while fasting and praying in the mountains. He knew that his message of repentance could cost him his head one day, but his worst struggle was in laying his family on the altar. As he wept, he wrote these words:

> Well, I pledge my head to heaven for the
>   gospel.
> And I ask no man on earth to fill my needs.
> Like the sparrow up above, I am enveloped in
>   His love,
> And I trust Him like those little ones He feeds.
>   (Matt. 6:25-26, 33)

> Well, I pledge my wife to heaven for the
>   gospel.
> Though our love each passing day just seems
>   to grow.
> As I told her when we wed, I'd surely rather be
>   found dead,
> Than to love her more than the one who saved
>   my soul. (Matt. 10:37; Luke 18:29-30)

> *Chorus:*
> I'm your child, and I wanna be in your family
>   forever.
> I'm your child, and I'm gonna follow you no
>   matter.
> Whatever the cost, well I'm gonna count all
>   things loss. (Phil. 3:7-8)

Well, I pledge my son to heaven for the gospel.
Though he's kicked and beaten, ridiculed and
    scorned.
I will teach him to rejoice and lift a thankful,
    praising voice,
And be like Him who bore the nails and
    crown of thorns. (Matt. 5:10-12)

Chorus

Well, I've had my chance to gain the world
    and to live just like a king,
But without Your love it doesn't mean a thing!
    (Matt. 16:26)

Oh, no matter whatever the cost, well I'm
    gonna count all things loss,
Oh, no matter whatever the cost, well I'm
    gonna count all things loss.

Well, I pledge my son . . . I pledge my wife . . .
    I pledge my head to heaven.
I pledge my son . . . I pledge my wife . . .
I pledge my head to heaven for the gospel.

What a challenge! Another song by Keith Green
that has motivated me in my personal witness is
"Asleep in the Light." The message of this song
should continually haunt the lukewarm church of
the twentieth century.

Do you see, do you see all the people sinking
   down?
Don't you care, don't you care? Are you gonna
   let them drown?
How can you be so numb not to care if they
   come?
You close your eyes and pretend the job's
   done.

"Oh bless me Lord, bless me Lord."
You know it's all I ever hear.
No one aches, no one hurts, no one even sheds
   one tear.
But He cries, He weeps, He bleeds, and He
   cares for your needs,
And you just lay back and keep soaking it in!
Oh, can't you see it's such sin?

'Cause He brings people to your door
And you turn them away, as you smile and say,
"God bless you, be at peace," and all heaven
   just weeps.
'Cause Jesus came to your door.
You've left Him out on the streets.

Open up, open up, and give yourself away.
You see the need, you hear the cries, so how
   can you delay?
God's calling, you're the one, but like Jonah
   you run.
He's told you to speak but you keep holding it in.

Oh, can't you see it's such sin!

The world is sleeping in the dark that the
    church just can't fight,
'Cause it's asleep in the light.
How can you be so dead when you've been so
    well fed?
Jesus rose from the grave, and you, you can't
    even get out of bed.
Oh, Jesus rose from the dead.
Come on, get out of your bed!

How can you be so numb not to care if they come?
You close your eyes and pretend the job's done.
You close your eyes and pretend the job's done.
Don't close your eyes, don't pretend the job's
    done.

Come away, come away, come away with Me,
    my love.
Come away from this mess, come away with
    Me, my love.

Some have labeled contemporary Christian
music as "insipid, flabby, anemic, spiritually bank-
rupt."[15] But these adjectives in no way describe the
message and life-style of Keith Green. Perhaps his
ministry could better be described as "a voice of
one crying in the wilderness."

Convicted at one point that the Christian music
industry was charging more than necessary for

tapes and records, Green began to advertise his tapes for "whatever you can afford." To this day the weary pilgrim who is short of cash can write for one of his tapes for the price of the postage stamp.

Others would question the lasting value of spiritual decisions made at a concert, but the fruit of Green's ministry has remained, with many missionaries tracing their call to the ministry of Keith Green.

In a local ministry, music can be used in many ways. When challenging people in the area of evangelism, "Asleep in the Light" can reinforce the impact of a spoken message. Other songs can be used to inspire worship.

PHIL KEAGGY
The following songs by Phil Keaggy could be used to drive home the atrocity of abortion and the Christian's perspective on adversity.

LITTLE ONES

Chorus:
Who will speak up for the little ones, helpless
and half abandoned?
They've got a right to choose life they don't
want to lose;
I've got to speak up, won't you?

Equal rights, equal time for the unborn children.

Their precious lives are on the line
Oh, how can we be rid of them?
Passing laws, passing out bills and new amend-
ments.
Pay the cost and turn about and face the
young defendants.

Chorus

Many come and many go, conceived but not
delivered.
The toll is astronomical! Oh, how can we be
indiff'rent?
Little hands, little feet; tears for Him who
made you.
Should all on earth forsake you now yet, He'll
never forsake you.

Chorus

Forming hearts, forming minds; quenched
before awakened.
For so many delivered crimes the earth will
soon be shaken.
Little hands, little feet, tears for Him who
made you.
Should all on earth forsake you now yet, He'll
never forsake you.

Chorus

DISAPPOINTMENT

Disappointment—HIS appointment, change
one letter
Then I see, that the thwarting of my purpose is
God's better choice for me.
His appointment must be blessing, though it
may come in disguise
For the end from the beginning, open to His
wisdom lies.
Disappointment—HIS appointment, whose?
The Lord's who loves me best,
Understands and knows me fully, who my
faith and love would test
For like loving, earthly parent, He rejoices
when He knows
That His child accepts unquestioned all that
from His wisdom flows

Disappointment—HIS appointment,
No good thing will He withhold, from denials
oft we gather
Treasures of His love untold.
Well, He knows each broken purpose leads to
fuller, deeper trust.
And the end of all His dealings, proves our
God is wise and just
Disappointment—HIS appointment, Lord, I
take it then as such,
Like the clay in hands of potter, yielding
wholly to Thy touch.

All my life's plan is Thy molding, not one single choice be mine.
Let me answer unrepining, Father, not my will but THINE.

Again, think of the impact these lyrics can have on young minds. Music is a major part of the youth culture. Thus, young people will hear these messages again and again as they enjoy the music. I firmly believe that replacing songs like "Born to Be Wild" and "I Can't Get No Satisfaction" with sermons in song such as "Asleep in the Light" was a major impetus to my spiritual growth. Oh, the potential that lies here for helping to reach a world of lost youth and baby boomers!

THE RESURRECTION BAND

The Resurrection Band, or Rez Band, was one of the first Christian bands to target the heavy metal crowd. Although other groups have followed, the servant heart and ministry base of this band command the respect of those who might otherwise cringe at their music.

With four children and many years of ministry experience behind them, Glenn and Wendi Kaiser can hardly be discounted as "young believers" (see 1 Tim. 3:6). In fact, an inquiry into their lives reveals that they are more wrapped up in the daily ministry of their inner-city Chicago church than the world of concerts, contracts, and tape sales.

When Christians found that Chicago's Uptown

neighborhood was devoid of a visible evangelical ministry, Jesus People USA (JPUSA) took root and began to target street people. By 1974 they were feeding two hundred street people daily as well as visiting prisons, hospitals, nursing homes, and centers for the handicapped. Today, members of JPUSA also teach night classes on discipleship, Bible study, cults, and witnessing.

Lyricist and singer Glenn Kaiser and drummer John Herrin are elders of the Christian community JPUSA. Glenn serves as the primary pastor and teacher; John Herrin oversees their business affairs. Stu Heiss and bassist Jim Denton serve as deacons.

"We're probably the most unlikely group of people that could be brought together in a rock 'n' roll band," says Glenn Kaiser. "I bet you could spend a whole day with each of us, doing what we do around here, and never suspect that we were in a band."[16]

Singer Wendi Kaiser echoes the group's ministry mentality: "If music died for us tomorrow, we would still be ministers. Another door of service and evangelism would open up."[17]

MYLON LEFEVRE AND BROKEN HEART

"When we first got together, the music was so bad that we didn't have any problem at all with idolatry," Mylon jests. "We began playing for free in a church gym. We played in a Methodist church. There were three people the first week. But the three became crowds, and we were there for five weeks. There were so many people getting saved, we had to keep moving, and we moved to a larger church. We saw 2,400 kids saved in the first year and a half."[18]

Mylon takes Broken Heart's ministry seriously. It's not just thinking up pretty tunes and finding words that rhyme. "We start writing our songs with fasting and prayer. As we look into the Word we ask God to show us a topic He'd like us to write about, and to inspire us by the Holy Spirit. Each one of our songs comes from the Bible. I can give you a specific Scripture on every song we've ever sung."[19]

Mylon's strategy is to give people enough Scripture and preaching ("Faith comes by hearing") during a concert that they can make an intelligent decision for Christ by the conclusion. The result? By 1989 his ministry was communicating with 160 thousand people who had indicated decisions at Broken Heart concerts.[20] Now their ministry has expanded beyond doing concerts to handling such responsibilities as answering the approximately five thousand letters that arrive monthly.

A family man in his mid-forties, on the road playing 150 shows a year, Mylon often grows weary from the battle. So why keep up the pace? "At the risk of oversimplifying things, it's the goodness of God that keeps me going," Mylon testifies. "If I was doing this for anybody other than the Son of God, I would have quit."[21]

As you can see, many of the artists who are in contemporary Christian music are there to minister—but the impact of these musical ministers can be fully appreciated only when they are seen in action among the groups they target. I have actually seen all these groups in concert. I have witnessed first-hand their impact on the teenagers whom I have brought to the concerts, and I have experienced the work of God in my own life as a result of what I saw and heard. Because of this, I view these ministries as more than simply alternatives to secular music. For those seeking to minister to the same target groups with the strategy of the apostle Paul, using such music becomes more than merely a live option. It becomes a moral imperative. I will address this more in the final chapters.

15

TAKING IT TO THE CHURCH

If you want to reach young people in this country,
write a song, don't buy an ad.
sociologist Serge Denisoff[1]

James Tucker is a sincere pastor. He preaches the
Word, witnesses to the lost, and shepherds the
flock. But Reverend Tucker has a serious blind
spot, an overlooked detail that erects a wall between him and the people he so desperately wants
to reach. He dresses in the English styles of the late
1700s, right down to the powdered wig.

His message is on target and his heart genuine,
but his appearance sends out confusing messages.
Those who have grown up under his ministry understand his desire to be holy and separate from the
world's styles. In fact, they have grown to appreciate the difference between the church and the
world. Still, Tucker confuses non-Christians. They
wonder if, in becoming a Christian, God will
require them to dress like Reverend Tucker. Some
Christians presume that because of his antiquated

dress, he can't relate to where they live. The youth just think he's weird.

Sadly, Reverend Tucker can't see his problem. He writes off the slim crowds and lack of response as evidence of the hardness of the world, never suspecting that people may be rejecting the wine merely because of the wineskin.

Find this story hard to believe? OK. It's pure fabrication. Or is it? If we merely changed the blind spot from 1700s dress to late 1800s or early 1900s musical styles, we might be right on target.

While we take great pains to keep our coats, ties, and slacks consistent with current styles (what pastor wears wide collars and polyester leisure suits in the early nineties?), we think nothing of clothing our worship in styles a century out of date.

To better clarify the issue, let us distinguish two broad approaches to ministry.

THE FORTRESS MENTALITY
The first approach is an extension of what one author has dubbed "the fortress mentality."[2] Ministers with this approach build physical and cultural walls within which the church is shielded from the world, and the world from the church. For this group, evangelism is not venturing out on the pagan's turf to relate to him. Rather, evangelism consists of evangelizing on the cultural and physical turf of the church, charging those in the pews to repent.

Occasionally, some in the vast crowd of

unchurched pagans will spot a nervous head pop-
ping up above the fortress wall, beckoning, "Come
and join us!" But pagans aren't interested in going
to church. They are too comfortable on their own
turf. Besides, they are too busy.

So we sit comfortably in our fortress, surrounded
by our Christian friends and Bible seminars, measuring success by how well we keep the fortress in
order and whether or not we reach the end of our
lives without making any major mistakes. In actual-
ity, staying pure from the sin of the world *is* important, but this does not encompass the totality of our
calling. God never called us to merely hold down
the fort; he called us to storm the heights.

THE MISSIONARY MENTALITY

We are called to be fishers of men, and good fisher-
men don't busy themselves on the shore, occasionally beckoning the fish to jump up on the dry land
with them. Instead, they study fish, learn what fish
like to eat, and launch their boats into the water
with the fish. This is what we call "the missionary
mentality." To see how this mentality applies to our
music, we must first of all educate ourselves in the
basics of missions strategy.

"Missionary Strategy: 101." For those of us
ministering in our native culture, let's imagine for
a moment that God has called us to a foreign tribe
in Brazil, South America, and we have recently
arrived with our team on the field. Deployed in a
remote, unreached village, we begin to debate

over strategy. One member of the team is convinced that the tribe's language and dress are inferior to ours, and the "natives" should be brought up to our cultural level in order to become Christians (sort of a "Real Christians Wear Ties" philosophy). Others on the team argue that Jesus adopted the dress and language of first-century Jewish culture, and if we are to follow in his steps, we must do the same.

In the former approach we impose Western culture on the people of the tribe, demanding life-style changes never required by God's Word. In the latter, we introduce the unchanging gospel to the culture, allowing the extrabiblical cultural trappings to assume their own forms, those most meaningful to the tribal people. When we allow a church's expression of Christianity to be tailored by the individual culture, then allow it eventually to be led by the people of that culture, we have built an "indigenous" church.

As much as we like praying in our own language, sitting in pews, and wearing a new Spring dress on Easter, we must recognize these practices for what they are: meaningful within our culture, possibly meaningless in another culture, and certainly not biblically mandated.

Those who aspire to be involved in cross-cultural work must radically evaluate their methodology in the light of Scripture. They must be willing to jettison their extrabiblical baggage, no matter how precious or meaningful that baggage may be within their home culture, to reach those in a foreign culture who may not respond to these forms.

Now, let's get back to Brazil. We decide that as a team we must learn their language and communicate the gospel using illustrations and analogies that are meaningful to the Brazilians. We resolve to de-Westernize our faith as we plant a truly indigenous church. We decide that to do otherwise would put us in the same category with the church of the Middle Ages, which imposed the Latin liturgy on European countries, thus alienating the masses from meaningful worship.

This, historically, is the realization that has come to those involved in missions: to truly evangelize a culture, you need to understand that culture, learn the language and customs, and approach the people in ways they will understand.

Unfortunately, what has become obvious to many missionaries concerning language and other forms of evangelization has not come so quickly with regard to music. According to Hustad, "Armed with the Sankey hymnals of their Anglo-American tradition, they translated our gospel songs into a thousand or more languages. Except for the Bible itself, no single body of literature has so completely circumvented the world, invading all cultures."[3]

As sincere as these efforts to export Western hymnody were, the wisdom gleaned from decades of missionary practice reveals some serious flaws. First, foreign styles inhibit people's ability to freely express their faith.[4] They should not be required to jump a cultural hurdle in order to worship.

According to missions professor R. LaVerne Morse,

> *In many parts of Asia, I have observed that non-Westernized nationals suffer culture shock when they are subjected to long periods of unfamiliar musical systems. This is true in China, Burma, northern Thailand, and Laos according to my personal experiences in these places. There is an immediate psychological reaction of culture shock that makes the Western Christian music a barrier rather than a bridge to the communicating of the message of Christ.[5]*

An old man in Chad, Africa, said, "I want to become a Christian, but do I have to learn your music?"[6]

Second, the original meaning of the hymns often is lost in the translation process. Again quoting Hustad, "When our hymn tunes are wedded to some of the world's 'tonal' languages, it has been discovered that our melodic progressions can completely reverse the meaning of a word or phrase."[7]

In summary, according to missionary music specialist Albert W. D. Frieson, this importation of Western hymn styles "has been detrimental to evangelism, the growth of an indigenous understanding of Christianity, and an independent Christian church in these cultures." The dominant approach today is to establish an indigenous hymnody.[8]

T. W. Hunt, professor of church music at Southwestern Baptist Theological Seminary and a leading authority in music missions has concluded: "Surely there can be no question that the only viable music for unreached peoples is their own."[9] In other words, the approach of Luther, Watts, Wesley, and others was more than just a good idea. It was sound missionary strategy. Missionaries who have encouraged indigenous styles of worship report enthusiasm and meaningful worship on the part of the people.[10] They recognize that music is not a side issue in missions. Using this medium effectively can greatly enhance mission work. Two Christians in Japan reported, "In Japan, music . . . attracts more unsaved than any other facet of the church program. . . . Our Christmas music program drew two hundred. An average evening attendance is about thirty."[11]

Phillip Anderson of the Philippines stated that music is "our best method of attracting people to services".[12] Another person from Japan stated, "If you know music, you will be able to communicate through this medium at least two years before you will ever be able to communicate effectively by speaking, preaching, or teaching in Japanese."[13] Furthermore, according to Hunt, "Indigenous expressions will evangelize more successfully, and the results will be more lasting."[14]

When Bill and Dellana O'Brien, missionaries to Indonesia, searched for a key to unlock the hearts of their people, they found that their musical performances failed to communicate and evoke commitment. So they began to experiment with classical Javanese and Balinese dance forms and native musical systems to portray Bible stories. The response was "overwhelming." The presentation exposed 25,000 viewers to the gospel in the first year.[15]

Of course, some would object, Won't the indigenous music have bad associations with pagan worship? Some music might, but this question reflects a misunderstanding of most cultures. Granted, one beat or style may be used exclusively for pagan worship and be considered inappropriate for Christian worship. However, other beats or styles within the tribe may be associated with weddings, working in the fields, rowing, happiness, or deep emotion. These styles bring up no images of demon worship. They simply represent the musical language of the people.

How then do missionaries determine what is appropriate for a tribe and what is not? In the context of choosing styles for urban areas, Hunt suggests: "What the missionary must discover is simply what is life to the nationals, where they are most likely to express intimacy. . . . What music do they sing in the kitchen or at leisure? They may prefer the study of Western music, but what would they play on the record player in their most relaxed moments?"[16]

Again, the spiritually mature among the target group will be best qualified to make these decisions. Delbert Rice, missionary to the Philippines, distributed mimeographed copies of potential worship songs to test them for effectiveness as indigenous hymnody. If a song was requested frequently in congregational worship, if it was sung on the mountain trails or in the fields, it was accepted. "If not," said Rice, "it must be considered as stillborn and buried regardless of the amount of precious love and labor that went into its development and birth."[17] This is an excellent example of the missionary mentality: ruthlessly discarding what took great pains to produce because of its ineffectiveness within the culture one is called to reach.

THE MISSIONARY MENTALITY APPLIED IN THE WEST

Now let's relocate our vantage point. Rather than being in America observing a foreign culture, we will be in a foreign culture from which we will view the American scene. Imagine, if you can, that rather than spreading westward from Jerusalem, the gospel primarily spread eastward in those early centuries, finding fertile soil in what we now call China and India. Let's imagine further that we are with a team of missionaries from China, sent to reach the pagan hordes of late twentieth-century America, who have yet to hear the gospel. There is no Bible in English, no historic church architecture, no rich heritage of Western hymnody.

We search for potential tools that have the attention of the people and find videotapes used extensively. Although 90 percent of these tapes communicate non-Christian values (what values would we expect non-Christians to communicate?), we find no reason not to plunder the devil for this useful tool and redeem it from its servitude to evil. Thus, we begin producing teaching videos and films that communicate Christian values and teaching.

Wishing to plant an indigenous church, we adopt the missionary mentality, place ourselves in the Americans' shoes, and try to determine the most appropriate forms in which to couch their hymnody. Traditional Chinese hymns are ineffective. Americans can't seem to relate to what we Chinese recognize as "good music."

Instead, we find a very musical culture that enjoys a variety of styles. Through our research we find that rock (including pop) is by far the most popular style,[18] capturing 50 percent of all record sales, the rest being divided between the rock derivatives disco and soul, then country, middle-of-the-road, jazz, and classical.[19]

Still, our concern is not so much what appeals on a national level as what appeals to the smaller segment we are targeting. So we immerse ourselves into a small, suburban town and begin our search for the music of the common person. We note the radio stations to which they awaken, the tunes they hum in the car, the songs they exercise to, and the bands that provide a backdrop for their work and play. Sure, many of the songs have non-Christian content. But what would we expect? They are non-Christians!

All of the forms are rather bizarre to us, but as we grow in our understanding of the culture we begin to see fruit. We work closely with the "natives" to determine which styles they feel would best function to express praise to God, to edify one another, and to present salvation to the lost. The consensus is that, in this region, the softer, more mellow forms of rock are more conducive to worship. Other forms such as soul, rap, or classical could well be used for concerts to target subgroups or offer listening alternatives. Had we chosen another region, we may have selected music with more of a country or soul flavor. It all depends on the people.

Is this really so peculiar a scenario? As a matter of fact, the statistics of music presented were those recorded in the 1980 edition of the *Contemporary Music Almanac*. If we were missionaries to the fictitious suburban town, which had its own very definite musical preference, which styles would we choose? Surely we would not research the history of this people's music and seek to resurrect a style that had lost its popular appeal generations earlier.

In choosing styles of music appropriate for the American church, the confusing factor is no longer so much the evils of rock, for rock in its various forms has pretty well established itself in many regions as the music of choice for the common people today. When people hear it in the grocery store, exercise to it in the gym, or wake up to it in the morning, they don't associate it with evil. Sure, some have used it for evil, but most associate the theme from *Rocky* with motivation to exercise, other songs with adventure, some with friendship, others with love.

The truly confusing factor in reaching the pagan people in America is our heritage of Christian music. Because of our rich heritage of hymnody, we are tempted to classify only these styles as sacred and anything else as secular. In doing this, we forget that the styles of our traditional hymns were once the popular styles of the world. Hustad argues that we erred in exporting the style of Sankey across the globe, regardless of culture. If so, have we also erred in retaining musical forms that worked in the past but have lost their meaning through years of change?

Just as our tribe in Brazil differs from people in a contemporary American culture, so the America of the past differs from the America of the present. As L. P. Hartley put it in the novel *The Go-Between*, "The past is a foreign country: they do things differently there."[20] Evangelistic worship forms that were indigenous to late nineteenth-century American culture may not be indigenous to late twentieth-century American culture. We must keep our fingers on the pulse of our society if we are convinced that indigenous forms are best for evangelism.

TRADITIONS: GOOD AND BAD

I don't wish to be misconstrued as advocating the abolition of hymns and a second round of organ demolitions. If we forget our heritage, we have lost something precious. A week seldom passes that I do not find myself singing Luther's majestic "A Mighty Fortress Is Our God." As I sing, I can almost hear the sound of the stocky German's lute reverberating off of castle walls as he joyously played and sang praises at the table with his friends. For a brief moment I am wearing Luther's shoes: condemned by the pope, expelled from the church, living in exile—but, by my discovery of justification by faith, I have been set free indeed. We dare not forget our heritage, and the music of Luther can help us remember.

However, if I think "A Mighty Fortress" will affect the average American the way it affects me, I have yet to understand my culture. Even within the church, the hymn often requires explanation to have its full impact. Among the pagan people, who may not know Martin Luther from Martin Luther King, Luther's "bulwark never failing" may have little or no meaning. It certainly is unlikely they will ever sing it in the shower.

Of course, there is nothing wrong with tradition, in and of itself. Traditions are good if they continue to have meaning within a culture. But let us not forget the seven last words of the church: "We never did it that way before." Authors Gordon L. Borror and Ronald B. Allen write, "History indicates that the [church] body that canonizes musical form and style begins to 'fossilize' right there."[21] Methods that worked in the past often become ineffective— yet we continue to use them because they are safe and comfortable, because we are suspicious of new-fangled methodology, or just because we are set in our ways.

J. David Stone shares a humorous experience that well illustrates the stubbornness of traditions that have lost their meaning:

> *At one old Methodist church I visited, worship always included the recitation of the Apostle's Creed. When the congregation stood to say the Creed, however, they all turned around and faced the back of the church. When it was over, they turned back around and sat down.*
>
> *Weird tradition,* I thought. But after some check-ing I discovered that, earlier in the century, when the church had had no books, they hung the Apostles' Creed on the balcony; worshipers consequently had to turn around and read it back there. By the time the balcony came down—and the Creed with it—the habit was just too firmly entrenched to change.[22]

"Onward Christian Soldiers" may have trum-peted a clarion call to the age for which it was writ-ten. However, it was the secular society that placed upon the march style the feeling of urgency, the association with going to war—but styles changed, as did their associations. Now the very song that challenged generations past to take up their weapons and march elicits yawns from contemporary youth. No matter how convincingly the voice of tradition may cry out in our hearts that this is the best, most effective music, there is no way that nineteenth- or early twentieth-century styles can be considered indigenous to the unbelievers of the late twentieth-century Western culture.

THE BOTTOM LINE

The styles that have captured the ears of our culture today—the styles that wake people up, make them laugh, relax them after a hard day at work, or call atrophied muscles to action at the spa—are seldom heard in the church. The styles we use in the church are the ones that made nineteenth-century people weep, laugh, relax, or report for duty. How odd. We are scratching people of the 1800s right where they itch.

We are doing all of this while we have within reach one of the most powerful tools imaginable for impacting our nation for Christ. Sadly, most ministries have allowed this tool to gather dust in their bag of weapons, and thus a mere 10 percent of even the church population listens to Christian music outside of the worship service.[23]

Contemporary Christian music now outsells jazz and classical,[24] but we have yet to see it unleashed upon the world. The twin giants of tradition and cultural captivity have been allowed to keep a formidable armada in dry dock.

As long as the style used inside the fortress is left there by the great majority of our churchgoers, and never picked back up until church resumes the next Sunday, we are not edifying our people. Only the polite unbelievers will stay awake during worship. I have yet to find a person under forty (and few over forty) who chose traditional hymns in traditional hymnbook arrangements as their style of preference outside of the church setting.

Let's not fool ourselves into thinking that we are following in the footsteps of Luther, Watts, Wesley, Sankey, and Booth if our congregations do not find themselves humming our tunes at work and playing our tapes during the week. Paul set aside many personal preferences and became all things to all people in order to reach them with the gospel. We have been content to become some things to some people, or worse, have expected all people to become all things to us. As a consequence, our ministries suffer.

As John R. W. Stott says in *Christian Mission in the Modern World,*

> *Our congregations demand from every new member not only a conversion but also a change in culture. [The new member] has to abandon some of his contemporary behavior and to accept the older patterns prevalent among the majority of the congregation. The new Christian has to learn the old hymns and to appreciate them. He has to learn the lan-*

guage of the pulpit. . . . In brief, he has to step back two generations and undergo what one may call a painful cultural circumcision.[25]

Some innovative American churches, aware of the cultural fortress that alienates large segments of our population from the church, have chosen to adopt the missionary mind-set and use musical forms most easily understood by their target audience. Eastside Foursquare Church in Kirkland, Washington, exploded from a few attendees to nearly four thousand in ten years. What part did their music play in this phenomenal growth? According to Pastor Doug Murren, "Unchurched baby boomers will be attracted to a church that is comfortable with their music style and has familiar sounds. In other words, they will be drawn to music with a contemporary sound."[26] (For further examples of growing churches using contemporary formats, see the appendix.)

While pop music has caught the imagination and dreams of a generation, the church at large merely dabbles with an occasional contemporary format. We are using deep-sea gear to pull the drain out of the bathtub. We are kidding ourselves when we think what appeals to us appeals to everyone. All too often we view ourselves as giving men and women a contemporary challenge to believe the claims of Christ, when actually they must struggle to see past our dated forms. Every time they look at us, they have trouble seeing past the powdered wig.

The bottom line was well expressed by producer, musician, and composer Reed Arvin when he wrote,

> *For the music minister attempting to make good his promise to reach out to the unsaved world . . . conventional music ministry approaches become less and less relevant to an audience that no longer even understands the vocabulary of faith. The truth is that we have been singing lovely songs to ourselves, and the world not only hasn't been listening, it hasn't even known we've been singing.*[27]

16

TAKING IT TO THE WORLD

*Give me the music of a nation and I will change the
mind of that nation.*

Plato[1]

A WORLDWIDE PHENOMENON
John Joyce is my hero. In charting the course of his
life, he determined to find an unreached people
group so remote that, were he not to go to them,
they probably would never hear the gospel. His
choice? The Fulani people of Burkina Faso in West
Africa. To see these people, fly east from the United
States, then look out your right window after you
see the sands of the Sahara Desert. The land is
harsh. The religion, Islam.

The Fulani are poor. They have no Bibles. What
they *do* have are radios—and many of them like
Michael Jackson.

Surprised? While rock was in its infancy, some
dismissed it as a passing fancy, not to be taken seriously. Today it has become what Hustad dubs "the
prevailing aesthetic of much of the Western
world."[2] Classical music is an elitist art. Pop, rock,

and their various forms such as soul and rap domi-
nate the airwaves and tape sales.

Besides tape sales and air play, another way to
judge a music style's popularity is to note the top
money-makers among entertainers. *Forbes* magazine's forty highest paid entertainers for the years
1989 and 1990 included nineteen music performers. The top five of these were Michael Jackson
(grossing $100 million), the Rolling Stones ($88
million), New Kids ($78 million), Madonna ($62
million), and Paul McCartney ($45 million).[3]

But rock's vast market extends beyond the borders
of the Western world. Mick Jagger's solo tour in 1988
included twenty-three concerts in Australia, as well
as concerts in New Zealand and Indonesia.[4] His
eight-show solo tour of Japan sold out in a matter of
hours, with fans paying an average price of approximately $50 in U.S. currency.[5] Michael Jackson's
1987–1988 tour took in fifteen countries on three
continents with a total attendance of 4.4 million
fans. [6] From August 1987 to January 1989, his *Bad*
album sold over 19 million units, with 12.5 million
of these purchased outside of the United States. It hit
the top of the charts in over twenty-five countries,
including Greece, Israel, Japan, Brazil, Hong Kong,
Spain, Austria, Italy, Denmark, France, and Germany.[7] *Newsweek*, reporting on the phenomenon in
Ethiopia, spoke of "thousands of young Africans who
have found a pop messiah in Michael Jackson. . . .
In the capital's marketplace, Jackson's androgynous
image is everywhere: on posters, T-shirts, souve-

nirs. . . . Taxis blare his music; weddings and funerals throb to his rhythms."[8]

On a recent trip to Eastern Europe, I was amazed to hear American top-forty music played in English, in taxis and hotels everywhere, even in a small-town market. According to Paul Borthwick, "Seventy percent of the songs played on Brazilian radio are in English."[9] A journalist in Indonesia recently published research showing Indonesian youth to be more interested in Michael Jackson than in Mohammed. The authorities promptly threw the journalist in jail. The youth, however, stayed tuned in to Jackson.[10]

Contemporary American and European music has become the chosen style of significant population segments worldwide. What does this mean for the Christian musician whose heartbeat extends beyond the borders of his own country?

IN THE FULLNESS OF TIME

The arrival of Jesus was in the fullness of time (Gal. 4:4), according to the Scriptures. He came at the appointed time. "God had prepared the whole world for the coming of His Son at this time in history," according to one commentator.[11] Although the immediate context may suggest the world being fully prepared by the law,[12] other aspects of God's timing were the completion of the prophetic timetable,[13] and the preparation of the world for the rapid spread of the gospel.[14]

The entire civilized world, with the exception of

the Far East, was united under Roman rule, bringing the needed peaceful climate. A common language, Greek, was used in the court and among the commoners, providing a universal medium. The Roman roads provided a transportation system of a higher quality than the world had ever seen. Philosophy had not provided the answers to life's deepest questions, and the dispersion of the Jews prepared the way with monotheistic teaching and the hope of a Messiah.[15] It is easy to understand how this fertile soil was "the fullness of time" for the Messiah to come.

Today we find ourselves in a similar situation. For decades the world has been slowly closing to the foreign missionary, but all of that is changing rapidly. The Iron Curtain is down, the atheistic philosophy behind Marxism has been weighed on the scales and found wanting, and much of the world is looking to the West for direction. Into this void, Christian "musicianaries" have found a niche. The road paved by American pop music is no longer the exclusive domain of the secular artists, transporting their hedonistic merchandise. Mylon LeFevre ministered recently in the Philippines and saw over ten thousand indicate decisions for Christ.[16]

Even before missionaries were allowed in Soviet bloc countries, Christian musicians were able to enter because of the nationals' appetite for Western pop music. Formed as an outreach to young people in Amsterdam, the Christian metal band No Longer Music recently toured such remote sites as

Kazakhstan and Kirghizia (both strong Muslim republics) and Siberia. Though warned to be low-key concerning their faith, they distributed Bibles and tracts and projected Russian translations of their songs in order to ensure good communication.[17]

More than two hundred individuals indicated decisions to receive Christ on this tour. The TV and radio interviews, the attention of the Soviet media, and an invitation back to Siberia demonstrate the openness to this form of ministry. "That part of the world is a field that's just ready to be harvested," said band leader David Pierce. "And we saw how with music you can go anywhere—rock 'n' roll is the music of the world."[18]

The band was formed as a part of Youth with a Mission's outreach to Amsterdam. This dynamic mission organization had 4,600 missionaries by 1986, making it the second largest foreign missions agency in the world. Danny Layman, director of YWAM in Hawaii, gives glowing reports of their extensive use of contemporary Christian music. Their band City Heat, from Hong Kong, recently attracted five thousand Indians in Madras, India. Layman has yet to see negative results. In fact, he knows many missionaries who felt their call to missions through the ministry of Keith Green.[19]

Of course, for ventures such as these to make a positive impact, the biblical principles of chapter 8 and the cross-cultural principles of chapter 15 must be carefully applied. If singers simply make a tour of a country with no thought for the vast cultural differences, no counsel from missionaries who have spent their lives working among the people, and bypassing input from national Christians, more harm than good may result. Remember, our goal is to present our Lord in a way that is intelligible and appealing to the culture we are trying to reach. To push our music on others, assuming that all people respond well to Western music, is no better than our earlier approach with the Sankey hymnals.

Even before the fall of the Iron Curtain, Christian artists Scott Wesley Brown, Sheila Walsh, Bruce Carroll, and Paul Smith performed in Tallinn, Estonia, at a festival that drew fifteen thousand people. Sponsored by Outreach for Christ, local Baptist and Methodist churches, and "I Care" Ministries, the event was the first such event ever to be publicized in the USSR. More than two thousand indicated commitments to Jesus.[20] (Of course, only God knows how many of the decisions reported throughout this book were actual conversions. We can only note the immediate response and look for lasting fruit.)

Scott Wesley Brown has served from Central America to Africa, to Russia, and to Hungary through his "I Care" Ministry. Besides giving concerts, his burden is to equip nationals for their own music ministries. He helps them acquire the needed instruments, recording equipment, and spiritual depth so that their ministries will produce solid spiritual teaching as well as musical excellence. "My audiences overseas far exceed my audience size in

America," says Brown. "Obviously, contemporary Christian music is really impacting a lot of the world because right now there is an incredible interest in Western pop music."[21]

George Verwer founded and leads one of the world's largest missions organizations, Operation Mobilization. Having used contemporary Christian music rather extensively for many years, he reports that he has only seen people helped in their spiritual growth through it. "The church in Latin America is moving into contemporary music," reports Verwer. "Wherever the church is growing it is generally on the cutting edge of music."[22]

Dennis Agajanian, famous as "the world's fastest flat-pick guitar player," has visited such war-torn countries as Cambodia, Lebanon, Nicaragua, and Honduras. Why take the risk? Certainly a guitarist of his caliber could find more glamorous outlets for his talents. But Agajanian's seemingly reckless abandon is ignited by a burden. "In times of war and suffering," he explains, "people will become more open and receptive to the words of hope the gospel of Jesus Christ contains."[23]

This attitude epitomizes the missionary mind-set, not following the path of least resistance or the most likely market to generate a profit, but searching for the greatest need and using music as a tool to apply the Word of God. Pioneer missionary C. T. Studd put it well: "Some want to live within the sound of church or chapel bell. I want to run a rescue shop, within a yard of hell."[24]

The increasing worldwide popularity of music from the West is opening doors that were formerly closed to traditional ministry. It is time for us to take these avenues seriously—to train musicians, evangelists, and church planters in the Bible and cross-cultural communication and then enlist them for duty.

It's time for more seminaries to take contemporary Christian music seriously and to offer concentrations in using contemporary forms in worship and evangelism. It's time for churches to channel the musical interests of youth into meaningful ministry. Are there avenues of ministry in your church for kids who are skilled in playing keyboards or guitars? If not, they may find other, less noble outlets for their talents.

As for those whose gifts lie in areas other than music ministry, if the church is truly the body of Christ, then it is time for the rest of the body to support our evangelists and teachers who are exercising their gifts through the avenue of contemporary music. Music ministries desperately need the support of local churches—the prophets to keep them on track, the mercy-givers to understand the struggles inherent in their ministries, the prayer warriors to fight battles in heavenly places, and church leadership to provide oversight.

All too often, however, these contemporary musicians venture outside the fortress walls and realize that the world has no intention of visiting our fortress. With the burden of a lost world on their shoulders and the power of the Word in their hands, they use these new tools to carry the gospel back to the streets and try to make worship relevant to the common people. Sometimes the burden grows heavy and the weary soldiers return to the fortress for rejuvenation—only to find the drawbridge clanging shut before them and stones being launched in their direction from inside the fortress walls.

Christian music ministry is tough from two angles: the opposition of the devil and the condemnation of much of the church. "The toughest thing to do is to win souls and please saints at the same time."[25] But many persist because of a vision and a burden that won't go away.

Perhaps this book will provide a bit of encouragement to someone who has taken his or her light outside of the fortress of the church to the multitudes of people who grope in darkness. Perhaps it will challenge a Christian artist to reexamine his motives and methods in the light of Scripture. Perhaps it will convince a local church to take its music a little more seriously and to get in touch with where its people are musically.

It is my hope that this book will promote understanding in the difficult period of transition that has historically been characterized by division, confusion, and animosity between brethren. I close with the burden of Petra, expressed in the words to their song, "Back to the Street."

It's so easy to lose the burden, take our eyes off the fields,

Settle into apathy and forget what the harvest
 yields.
It's so easy to think we're finished with our
 labor for a while,
Kick back and let somebody else go the extra mile.

Jesus said, "Go into all the world:
Make disciples of all men."
We gotta go to the highways,
And compel them to come in.
As long as there's a tearful eye that cries alone
 at night,
As long as there's a weary soul ready to end
 the fight,
As long as there's an aching heart that still has
 strength to beat,
We gotta take this message
Back to the street!

It's so easy to stay untangled with ev'ryone
 else's life:
Don't get involved with strangers, don't get
 involved with strife.
It's so easy to save your own life, resting on
 what you've done,
But Jesus would leave the ninety-nine to try to
 save the one.
It's not easy to beat the system, it's not easy to
 face the heat,
But somebody's got to take this message
Back to the street.

Appendix

How Four Growing Churches use Contemporary Music

In an age when most American churches struggle to survive, some churches are experiencing explosive growth. Although none of the following churches would attribute their accomplishments solely to their use of music, all would attest to its centrality in their goals of reaching the lost and building up the saved.

This appendix gives thumbnail sketches of four growing churches and the ways in which they incorporate contemporary music into the life of their services and outreach.

But before you proceed, let me offer two warnings: (1) Worship forms are better caught than taught. Words grope futilely to express what can only be experienced. It is much better to visit (or at least listen to a cassette tape of) one of these church services than to request a written synopsis of their music program. (2) If one of these pastors relocated to your area, his music programs might take on a very different form. Remember, these churches are implementing musical forms that are well received in their geographic location with the people they are targeting. Nevertheless, a study of their innovations can open our eyes to possibilities outside the range of our own experience.

SECOND BAPTIST CHURCH[1]
Pastor: Dr. H. Edwin Young
Location: Houston, Texas
Growth: More than nine thousand joined in the past nine years; growth of more than four thousand in Sunday school attendance in the same period. Baptized more than 750 in 1989.

Formats: *Sunday Morning.* Focus on traditional hymns accompanied by organ, choir, and orchestra. Solos are usually contemporary.

Sunday Night. Focus on contemporary praise songs accompanied by guitars, keyboard (synthesizer), some brass, and drums. No choir. If hymns are mixed in, they are done in a contemporary style. Words to choruses are put on a big screen. No hymnbooks.

Specials. "Super Summer Sunday Nights." Summer of '91 had concerts by own church members and mini-dramas, followed by a fellowship time. Different each week (for example, pops concert by church orchestra, "Hurrah for Hollywood" by choir, purely secular music). Attended by two thousand to twenty-five hundred people each night.

Youth. Wednesday night "Solid Rock" ministry targeting high school and college students. About three hundred in attendance. A band composed of guitars (acoustic, electric, and bass), drums, keyboard, and several singers leads in upbeat praise and worship. Contemporary Christian music videos are run on a big screen as people enter and exit. Church also hosts concerts by such artists as Twila Paris, Rich Mullins, and Wayne Watson. Promotes contemporary Christian tapes in church bookstore and plays tapes prior to Sunday school. Also promotes teens going to area concerts of groups such as Petra.

EASTSIDE FOURSQUARE CHURCH[2]
Pastor: Doug Murren
Location: Kirkland, Washington. In 1979, nearly 95 percent of the city's population attended no church.
Target Group: Nominal and unchurched baby boomers.
Growth: From a few attendees in 1981 to nearly four thousand in 1990.

Music Strategy: (1) Research the styles most popular in the area and use these to reach the unchurched. (2) Constantly evaluate effectiveness and strive for excellence, since baby boomers respond to quality music. Pastor evaluates both content and quality of songs. "I frequently ask myself 'Is the music and worship time in our church services truly representative of the tastes and style of the people whom I'm called to lead?'"[3]

Formats: *Saturday Night and Sunday Morning Services*. Geared to unchurched and seekers. Prelude usually secular tunes such as James Taylor to help visitors feel "safe." One hymn with contemporary arrangement sung, followed by worship choruses, many of which are written by members of congregation. Led by contracted musicians (drums, bass, acoustic and electric guitars, two keyboard players). Lots of sequenced music for specials. About every other week a horn player is featured. Will often take a popular, secular song and rewrite lyrics. (Staff have found that permission to record such songs can be obtained quite easily, often free of charge.) According to pastor Murren, "We are quite comfortable with including rock-type music in our morning service."

Sunday Night. Adults meet in classes, youth have the sanctuary for "The Happening," a youth worship time where the music primarily runs to rock and rap styles. Incorporate secular songs with lyrics that can easily be changed to deliver a Christian message.

Special Performances. A few times per year bring in special contemporary Christian artists such as Phil Keaggy or Annie Herring (of The Second Chapter of Acts). Two musical outreaches per year. "We take contemporary songs from the 1960s through the 1980s and theme them to a script. Professional directors, musicians, and writers then take our team's ideas and put them to work for us." Performed by lay people in the church. The response?

"Overwhelming." Rarely advertise outside the church since the church members invite friends and sell programs out. "We have found that nearly half of the unchurched people in the area will come to a high-quality event that is intelligible to them."

WILLOW CREEK COMMUNITY CHURCH[4]
Pastor: Bill Hybels
Location: South Barrington, Illinois
Growth: In 1975 rented Willow Creek Movie Theater on Sundays to begin their church. Within fifteen years have exploded to a weekly attendance of more than fourteen thousand, making it the second largest church in America.

Philosophy of Music: Those interested in getting a behind-the-scenes look at Willow Creek's music programming should either attend their Church Leadership Conference (held three times yearly) or listen to cassettes of these sessions, which are available through the church. Here the seeker will find a distillation of practical wisdom gleaned from years of training, programming, and working with music teams.

For Willow Creek, no song is considered a filler; each has a purpose. Music is chosen for its ability to touch people, to make them think, ponder, question, or experience truth. The staff know which radio stations the unchurched listen to and what concerts they attend, and use the styles that move their target group.

Since worship can easily fall into a rut, each week is different both in order of service and in tone. If one service begins with high energy and excitement, the next may begin on a more mellow note.

Formats: *Seeker Services.* Two Saturday night services and two Sunday morning services. Since these services target the unchurched, they use popular styles that communicate to the typical twenty-five- to forty-five-year-old unchurched professional. All four services are identical. Accompanied twice a month by a forty-piece orchestra that includes strings, brass, woodwinds, piano, synthesizer, and percussion. The remaining two weeks alternate between a rhythm section (electric guitar, bass, drums, synthesizer, piano) and a studio band (rhythm section and brass). When a service theme is more majestic or "vertical," the orchestra is used. If a more informal atmosphere is called for, the other accompanists are used.

Although the order of service varies from week to week, a typical service might begin with congregational song (Willow Creek is selective as to which songs are appropriate for the congregation in a service for seekers). Second would come two specials— the first lighter, the second designed to gear down toward the message. Next would be a drama on the theme of the message, and then would come the message.

New Community. Wednesday and Thursday

night services; designed to build up the Christian. Musical style is contemporary and accompanied by the rhythm section. Order varies from week to week, but a service may begin with a prelude, then move into twenty to thirty minutes of worship with choruses. A few older songs in contemporary arrangements may be mixed in, as well as some choruses written by people of the church. The choruses usually revolve around the topic of the message, although they do stand on their own at times. A new chorus is introduced about once a month. After the worship time comes Family Concerns (issues in the church), the offertory (usually with one or two specials), and then the message.

Specials. Generally Willow Creek doesn't bring in outside artists for main services. Once or twice a year they have hosted such artists as Ken Medema or Chuck Girard for a mini-concert (about one half of the service). Church choir sings four or five times per year at the New Community service. The choir's main role, when it is used, is to assist in leading worship. Willow Creek does not use choirs on a regular basis, because the choral style is not popular among the general public.

High School Ministry. Tuesday evening "Student Impact" meeting, designed to attract and reach non-Christian teenagers. Uses secular music that has no questionable content, but may present a positive or thought-provoking message. Some youth present music by their own bands. In addition, speakers and bands use media, video, and drama.

Sunday evening youth meetings are designed for the Christian teenager and use contemporary praise and worship choruses, sometimes led by a band, with words on screen. The church has brought in bands, such as Rick Cua, but generally uses its own bands.

MOUNT PARAN CHURCH OF GOD[5]

Pastor: Dr. Paul Walker

Location: Atlanta, Georgia (Mount Paran meets in two locations but, for brevity's sake, we will focus on Mount Paran Central.)

Growth: Has grown from an average attendance of 3,231 in 1979 to 8,850 in 1989.

Constituency: Not primarily a baby boomer church. Pretty evenly divided among all ages.

Formats: *Sunday Morning.* 7:45 A.M. Chapel service. Liturgical charismatic service led by organist, worship leader, and soloist. Solos are contemporary (such as Sandi Patti or Steve Green songs with sound tracks).

9:00 A.M. and 11:00 A.M. services. Ninety-minute services, approximately half of which is devoted to praise through song. Led by worship leader, choir, and orchestra. Choir does primarily contemporary music such as "Holy of Holies" and "Come Before Him." A typical service may follow this order: prelude; call to worship (a full song); Scripture and prayer; traditional hymn; package of choruses (including a "chorus of the day," a new chorus that will be sung three consecutive Sundays so that the congregation will learn it); minister comes in on the last song and may lead in a few more; announcements (printed in bulletin, highlighted from pulpit); offering (choir sings); message; minister may lead spontaneously in a chorus.

Sunday Night. Much like the morning services, but more spontaneous and lively. More upbeat, with more drums, rhythm section, and clapping.

Wednesday Night Chapel Service. Appeals to senior adults. Use some Southern Gospel music.

Special Events and Target Ministries:

Youth. Although the church's own band leads praise times at their gatherings, Mount Paran also brings in Christian rock bands such as the Newsboys for Friday concerts. Many other outside concerts are promoted through the church. Youth choir sings contemporary music and sings at the Sunday evening service once a month.

Entire Church. Five to six times per year a guest artist will sing a couple of specials in the morning services and give the choir a day off. The artist also does a concert during the evening service. Mount Paran has used contemporary groups such as New-Song, the Gaithers, Truth, and Mylon LeFevre (using his slower songs for a more general appeal), and Southern gospel groups such as the Cathedrals and the Talleys.

Other. This church is interested in helping aspiring artists to develop their own music ministries.

NOTES

CHAPTER 1. THE CHRISTIAN MUSIC CONTROVERSY

1. See Appendix, "Willow Creek Community Church."
2. James Emery White, *Opening the Front Door: Worship and Church Growth* (Nashville, Tenn.: Convention Press, 1992), 83. John Bisagno puts it stronger—"Long-haired music, funeral dirge anthems, and stiff-collared song leaders will kill the church faster than anything in the world. Let's set the record straight for a minute. There are no great, vibrant, soul-winning churches reaching great numbers of people, baptizing hundreds of converts, reaching the masses that have stiff music, seven-fold amens, and a steady diet of classical anthems, none. That's not a few. That's none, none, none." John Bisagno, *How to Build an Evangelistic Church* (Nashville: Broadman, 1971), 13. As quoted by White, 84.
3. Russell Chandler, *Racing toward 2001* (Grand Rapids, Mich.: Zondervan Publishing House and San Francisco: Harper San Francisco, 1992), 299.
4. "Evangelism," Class notes from Dr. Roy Fish, Southwestern Baptist Theological Seminary.
5. Chandler, 299.
6. Elmer L. Towns, *Ten of Today's Most Innovative Churches* (Ventura, Calif.: Regal Books, 1990), 15.
7. Leonard J. Seidel, *Face the Music* (Springfield, Va.: Grace Unlimited Publications, 1988), 115.

CHAPTER 2. CHARGES OF HEALTH THREATS

1. See *Striving for Excellence* (Oakbrook, Ill.: Institute in Basic Life Principles, 1989), 12-13. See also Seidel, *Face the Music,* 146.
2. John Diamond, *Your Body Doesn't Lie* (New York: Warner Books, 1979). See also John Diamond, *The Life Energy in Music* (Valley Cottage, N.Y.: Archaeus Press, 1981).
3. Diamond, *Your Body Doesn't Lie,* 7, 9.
4. *Ibid.,* 159-167.
5. See Diamond, *Your Body Doesn't Lie,* 67, 76, 79, 81, 95, 126, 167.
6. "Student After Sit-Up Record," *Daily Citizen-News* (Dalton, Ga.: Associated Press).
7. Diamond, *Your Body Doesn't Lie,* 164.
8. Craig W. Fontaine and Norman D. Schwalm, "Effects of Familiarity of Music on Vigilant Performance," *Perceptual and Motor Skills* 49 (1979), 71-74.
9. Fontaine and Schwalm, *Perceptual and Motor Skills,* 71 (italics mine).
10. David W. Sogin, "Effects of Three Different Musical Styles of Background Music on Coding by College-Age Students," *Perceptual and Motor Skills* 67 (1988), 275-280.
11. Leon K. Miller and Michael Schyb, "Facilitation and Interference by Background Music," *Journal of Music Therapy* 26:1 (1989), 42-54.
12. *Striving for Excellence,* 13.
13. Gervasia M. Schreckenberg and Harvey H. Bird, "Neural Plasticity of Musculus in Response to

Disharmonic Sound," *Bulletin of the New Jersey Academy of Science* 32:2 (Fall 1987), 77-86.

14. Richard Lipkin, "Jarring Music Takes Toll on Mice," *Insight*, 4 Apr. 1988, 58.

15. According to Dr. Schreckenberg, this was merely a pilot study in need of much refining. The beats used had no rhythm; they were chaotic. (From conversation with Dr. Schreckenberg, 30 Aug. 1991.)

16. Catherine Joseph and A. K. Pal, "Effect of Music on the Behavioral Organization of Albino Rats Using the Operant Conditioning Technique," *Indian Journal of Applied Psychology* 19 (July 1982), 77-84.

17. Valerie N. Stratton and Annette H. Zalanowski, "The Relationship between Music, Degree of Liking, and Self-Reported Relaxation," *Journal of Music Therapy* 21:4 (1984), 184-192 (italics mine).

18. Stratton and Zalanowski, *Journal of Music Therapy*, 184-192.

19. Suzanne B. Hanser, "Controversy in Music Listening/Stress Reduction Research," *The Arts in Psychotherapy* 15 (1988), 211-217.

20. *Ibid.*, 214.

21. Maria R. Souza, Cecilia Camacho, and Sandra Tavares, *Psicologia* 11 (1985), 53-62.

22. Cupurso, Fisichelli, Gilman, Gutheil, Wright, and Paperte, *Music and Your Emotions* (Musical Research Foundation, Inc., 1952).

23. *Publisher's Weekly* 214 (4 Dec. 1978), 57.

24. John Ankerberg and John Weldon, *Can You*

Trust Your Doctor?: The Complete Guide to New Age Medicine and Its Threat to Your Family (Brentwood, Tenn.: Wolgemuth and Hyatt, 1991), 166.

25. Philip G. Zimbardo, in consultation with Floyd L. Ruch, *Psychology and Life,* 9th ed. (Glenview, Ill.: Scott, Foresman and Company, 1975), 47. Zimbardo wisely cautions us that "conclusions drawn from scientific experiments are only as sound as the data they are based on and the objectivity with which they are interpreted. We are bombarded by the media every day with purported 'scientific conclusions' whose worth we must be able to evaluate if we are to avoid falling into psychological 'traps.'"

26. Psychologists caution us to beware of the common fallacy of the "crucial experiment," which is declared with finality to prove a certain theory. See Robert B. Lawson, Steven G. Goldstein, and Richard E. Musty, *Principles and Methods of Psychology* (New York: Oxford University Press, 1975), 10.

27. Four insights offered by Dr. Henry Virkler, professor of psychology at Liberty University, should be considered by those who research in this area: (1) "Beware of generalizations that lump everyone together and don't recognize the individual differences with which God created us"; (2) "Examine research carefully, preferably firsthand, before accepting it as valid. Obtain counsel from a specialist in the area if you have

questions about how to interpret [research] or how to judge its validity"; (3) "Don't accept research as valid just because it agrees with your biases. Your biases and the research may both be wrong"; (4) "Recognize that our apprehension of truth is a continuing process. It's always easier to change our position in the light of new data if we haven't been overly dogmatic about the way we held to our former position." (From correspondence with Dr. Henry Virkler, May 1991.)

CHAPTER 3. CHARGES OF MORAL CORRUPTION

1. *Notice of Complaint against the Unrecognized Enemy in the Church* (Oakbrook, Ill.: Institute in Basic Life Principles, 1990), 15. See also, *What the Bible Has to Say about "Contemporary Christian" Music: Ten Scriptural Reasons Why the "Rock Beat" Is Evil in Any Form* (Oakbrook, Ill.: Institute in Basic Life Principles, 1990), 9-10.

2. Elizabeth F. Brown and William R. Hendee, "Adolescents and Their Music," *Journal of the American Medical Association* 262:12 (22–29 Sept. 1989), 1659-1663. See also rejoinders to this article in the *Journal of the American Medical Association* 263:6 (9 Feb. 1990), 812-813. Since the critics quoted a newspaper article rather than the actual study, we assume that their error lies in failing to study the primary document rather than purposefully misrepresenting the study.

3. *Today's Teens: A Generation in Transition* (Glendale, Calif.: The Barna Research Group, 1991), 31.

4. See Gilbert Rouget, *Music and Trance,* trans. Brunhilde Biebuyck (Chicago: The University of Chicago Press, 1985). Rouget's work is also helpful in evaluating the shortcomings of Rodney Needham's focus on percussion as having a universal connection with transition. See Rodney Needham, "Percussion and Transition," *Man* 2 (1967), 606-614, and Andrew Neher's claims that the impact of tribal beats can be explained in purely physiological terms: "Auditory Driving Observed with Scalp Electrodes in Normal Subjects," *Electroencephalography and Clinical Neurophysiology* 13 (1961), 449-451, and "A Physiological Explanation of Unusual Behavior in Ceremonies Involving Drums," *Human Biology* 34 (1962), 151-160. Rouget argues that if the trance were purely a physiological response to the beat, then the beat would affect all the participants in the ritual. But such is not the case. See his other arguments in this regard in Rouget, 169-176.

5. Ronald Allen and Gordon Borror, *Worship: Rediscovering the Missing Jewel* (Portland, Oreg.: Multnomah Press), 167.

6. Stanley Sadie, ed., "Jewish Music," *The New Grove Dictionary of Music and Musicians* (Washington, D.C.: McMillan, 1980), 9:632.

7. Roland H. Bainton, *Here I Stand: A Life of*

Martin Luther (Nashville, Tenn.: Abingdon, 1950), 161.

8. Al Menconi, *Today's Music: A Window to Your Child's Soul* (Elgin, Ill.: David C. Cook, 1990), 140.

9. *What the Bible Has to Say about "Contemporary Christian" Music,* 8, 11-12.

10. Personal interview with G. William Supplee (April 1991).

11. Rouget, *Music and Trance,* 90.

12. See Rouget, *Music and Trance,* 69, 75, 85, 113-114, 149, 312-313.

13. *Ibid.,* 73.

14. *Ibid.,* 149.

15. See F. F. Bruce, *The Epistle of Paul to the Romans* (Grand Rapids, Mich.: Eerdmans, 1963), 251, 253. See also John Murray, *The Epistle to the Romans* (Grand Rapids, Mich.: Eerdmans, 1959), 190-191. For helpful discussions of limitations on responsibilities of the stronger brother, see Carl F. H. Henry, *Christian Personal Ethics* (Grand Rapids, Mich.: Eerdmans, 1957), 420-436. See also J. Robertson McQuilkin, *Biblical Ethics* (Wheaton, Ill.: Tyndale House, 1989), 502-507.

16. Personal conversation with Al Menconi (10 June 1991).

17. Personal interview with Christian counselor Tim Gunter. (Summer, 1991)

18. *Ibid.*

19. See Appendix for examples.

CHAPTER 4. CHARGES OF WORLDLINESS

1. G. R. Beasley Murray, *Baptism in the New Testament* (Grand Rapids, Mich.: Eerdmans, 1962), 2-4.
2. Robert Haldane, *The Epistle to the Romans* (London: The Banner of Truth Trust, n.d.), 556.
3. F. F. Bruce, *The Epistles of John* (Grand Rapids, Mich.: Eerdmans, 1970), 60-61. Note also R. V. G. Tasker, *The New Bible Dictionary,* ed. J. D. Douglas (Grand Rapids, Mich.: Eerdmans, 1962), 1339: "Accordingly, worldliness is the enthronement of something other than God as the supreme object of man's interests and affections. Pleasures and occupations, not necessarily wrong in themselves, become so when an all-absorbing attention is paid to them."
4. I. Howard Marshall, *The First Epistle of John* (Grand Rapids, Mich.: Eerdmans, 1978), 143.
5. Warren Anderson, "Josh McDowell: Bridging the Gap," *Contemporary Christian Music* (June 1990), 36.

CHAPTER 5. CHARGES OF POOR AESTHETIC QUALITY AND A CAUTIONING INNER WITNESS

1. Donald Hustad argues for this functional approach to church music: "Church music has to be approached as a functional, instrumental art" and "music in the church being great art is irrelevant, in terms of what the western world considers great art. You must pull yourself apart from approaching church music as a free art or

as the best art" (interview, 14 April 1977, at Southern Baptist Theological Seminary in Louisville, Kentucky); quoted in Donald Paul Ellsworth, *Christian Music in Contemporary Witness* (Grand Rapids, Mich.: Baker Book House, 1979), 166.

2. Barry, Liesch, *People in the Presence of God* (Grand Rapids, Mich.: Zondervan, 1988), 196.
3. H. C. Leupold, *Exposition of the Psalms* (Grand Rapids, Mich.: Baker Book House, 1969), 14.
4. Missionaries Vida Chenoweth and Darlene Bee, at the time missionaries to New Guinea, addressed this problem in their article "On Ethnic Music," *Practical Anthropology* (Sept./Oct. 1968), 205-212: "Barriers in both language and music may be overlaid with ethnocentric prejudices, which can lead to unfortunate value judgments. Someone may say that a given people have no music or that their music is 'unmusical.' While well-intentioned, these judgments are rather like saying a people have no language or that their language is 'unlinguistic.' The first step in overcoming a music barrier is to recognize it objectively for what it is—an avenue of communication closed to the uninitiated outsider" (205). Warren Dwight Allen, in *Philosophies of Music History,* wrote that "we are getting away from attempts to distinguish 'superior' from 'inferior' phases of musical art in an evolutionary series. This means no abandonment of a belief in standards,

however; on the contrary, appreciation of music will be on a higher plane when we learn to recognize sincerity in musical art, regardless of classification, function, or epoch." (New York: Dover Publications, 1939), 146; quoted by Ellsworth, *Christian Music in Contemporary Witness*, 21.

5. This criticism, dated 1823, was quoted in the *Musical Times* (Oct. 1922), 733.

6. All quotes from M. D. Calvocoressi, *The Principles and Methods of Musical Criticism* (New York: Da Capo Press, 1979), 81-83.

7. Chenoweth and Bee, 206. "For one steeped in a single musical tradition, especially a tradition as highly developed as our Western tradition, it is very difficult to accept another music as legitimate expression. It seems to be more difficult for the Christian steeped in Western hymnology to recognize that another musical system can be equally meaningful."

8. Warren Anderson, "Josh McDowell: Bridging the Gap," *Contemporary Christian Music* (June, 1990), 36.

9. Cyril J. Barber, *A Minister's Library* (Grand Rapids, Mich.: Baker Book House, 1974), xi.

Chapter 6. Charges of Bad Associations, Questionable Motives, and Dangerous Leanings

1. William F. Arnt and F. Wilbur Gingrich, *A Greek-English Lexicon of the New Testament*

and Other Early Christian Literature (Chicago:
The University of Chicago Press, 1957), 220.

2. M. R. Vincent, *Vincent's Word Studies,* vol. 2
   (McLean, Virginia: MacDonald Publishing
   House, n.d.), 947. See also R. C. H. Lenski, *The
   Interpretation of St. Paul's Epistles to the
   Colossians, to the Thessalonians, to Timothy, to
   Titus and to Philemon* (Minneapolis, Minn.:
   Augsburg, 1937), 362: "What is said by Paul is
   that wickedness has many forms, every one of
   which is really wickedness and also appears so to
   men, and we are to keep away from every form
   that wickedness may assume." See also George
   Milligan, *St. Paul's Epistle to the Thessalonians*
   (Minneapolis, Minn.: Klock and Klock Christian,
   reprint, 1980), 77, and Leon Morris, *The
   Epistles of Paul to the Thessalonians* (Grand
   Rapids, Mich.: Eerdmans, 1956), 106.

3. See Dana Key, *Don't Stop the Music* (Grand
   Rapids, Mich.: Zondervan, 1989), 63.

4. Al Menconi, "Whose Records Should I Burn,
   Alice's or Amy's?" *Media Update* 6:3 (May/June
   1987), 5.

5. Key, *Don't Stop the Music,* 116.

6. David R. Breed, *The History and Use of Hymns
   and Hymn Tunes* (Tarrytown, N.Y.: Revell,
   1903), 268.

7. W. Y. Fullerton, *Charles H. Spurgeon, London's
   Most Popular Preacher* (Chicago: Moody Press,
   1966), 83.

8. Donald Hustad, *Jubilate! Church Music in the*

Evangelical Tradition (Carol Stream, Ill.: Hope, 1981), 95.

9. Hustad, *Jubilate!* 132.

10. "Christians who through Christ have died to the elements of the cosmos, no longer live 'in the cosmos' (Col. 2:20b), but have been completely freed from subjection to its precepts and constraints." J. Guhrt on *kosmos* in the *Dictionary of New Testament Theology,* ed. Colin Brown, vol. 1 (Grand Rapids, Mich.: Zondervan, 1975), 525.

11. R. V. G. Tasker, *New Bible Dictionary,* ed. J. D. Douglas (Grand Rapids, Mich.: Eerdmans, 1962), 1339.

Chapter 7. The Bible on Music

1. William F. Arnt and F. Wilbur Gingrich, *A Greek-English Lexicon of the New Testament and Other Early Christian Literature* (Chicago: The University of Chicago Press, 1957), 546.

2. *Dictionary of New Testament Theology,* ed. Colin Brown (Grand Rapids, Mich.: Zondervan, 1975).

3. Ralph H. Alexander, *Theological Wordbook of the Old Testament,* eds. R. Laird Harris, Gleason L. Archer Jr., and Bruce K. Waltke, vol. 1 (Chicago: Moody Press, 1980), 364-365.

4. J. Robertson McQuilkin, *Understanding and Applying the Bible* (Chicago: Moody Press, 1983), 255ff.

5. As quoted in Dan Peters, Steve Peters, and Cher

Merrill, *What about Christian Rock?*
(Minneapolis, Minn.: Bethany House, 1986),
100.

6. Paul Henry Lang, *Music in Western Civilization,*
700; cited by Donald P. Hustad, *Jubilate! Church
Music in the Evangelical Tradition* (Carol
Stream, Ill.: Hope, 1981), 33-34.

7. Robert M. Stevenson, *Patterns of Protestant
Church Worship* (Duke University Press, 1953), 152.

8. Stevenson, *Patterns of Protestant Church
Worship,* 151.

CHAPTER 8. BIBLICAL PRINCIPLES FOR MUSICIANS AND SPONSORS

1. Dave Geisler, "Musicianaries for Christ,"
Contemporary Christian Music (May 1990), 22.

2. Al Menconi, *Today's Music: A Window to Your
Child's Soul* (Elgin, Ill.: David C. Cook, 1990),
142.

3. R. C. H. Lenski, *The Interpretation of St. Paul's
Epistles to the Colossians, to the Thessalonians,
to Timothy, to Titus, and to Philemon*
(Minneapolis, Minn.: Augsburg, 1937), 184.

4. M. R. Vincent, *Word Studies in the New
Testament,* vol. 1 (McLean, Va.: MacDonald,
1888), 318.

CHAPTER 9. FROM EARLY CHANTS TO REFORMATION SONGS

1. Edward S. Ninde, *The Story of the American
Hymn* (Nashville, Tenn.: Abingdon, 1921), 94-97.

2. David R. Breed, *The History and Use of Hymns
and Hymn Tunes* (Tarrytown, N.Y.:Revell,
1903), 255.

3. Breed, *History and Use of Hymns*, 21-22.
4. *Ibid.*, 25.
5. Donald Paul Ellsworth, *Christian Music in Contemporary Witness* (Grand Rapids, Mich.: Baker Book House, 1979), 30.
6. Breed, *History and Use of Hymns*, 256.
7. Jane Stewart Smith, *The Gift of Music* (Wheaton, Ill.: Crossway Books, 1987), xix.
8. Karl Gustav Fellerer, *The History of Catholic Church Music*, translated by Francis A. Brunner (Baltimore: Helicon Press, 1961), 56.
9. Breed, *History and Use of Hymns*, 290.
10. *Ibid.*, 38-39.
11. Preserved Smith, *The Life and Letters of Martin Luther* (New York: Barnes and Noble, Inc. 1911, 1968), 346-347.
12. Smith, *The Life and Letters of Martin Luther*, 347.
13. Roland H. Bainton, *Here I Stand: A Life of Martin Luther* (Nashville, Tenn.: Abingdon, 1950), 267.
14. Paul Nettl, *Luther and Music*, trans. Frida Best and Ralph Wood, (Philadelphia: The Muhlenberg Press, 1948), 34.
15. Theodore Hoetty-Nickel, *Luther and Culture*, Martin Luther Lectures, vol. 4, (Decorah, Iowa: Luther College Press, 1960), 210.
16. Smith, *The Life and Letters of Martin Luther*, 231.
17. *Ibid*, 231.
18. Hoetty-Nickel, *Luther and Culture*, 174.

19. *Ibid.,* 174-175.
20. Richard Friedenthal, *Luther, His Life and Times,* translated by John Nowell (New York: A Helen and Kurt Wolff Book, Harcourt Brace Jovanovich, Inc., 1967), 464.
21. Hoetty-Nickel, *Luther and Culture,* 173-174.
22. *Ibid.,* 169.
23. Tilemann Heshusius, *Psalms of David;* cited by Koch, *Geschechte des Kirchenliedes und Kirchengesangs* (Stuttgart, 1867), 244; quoted by Hoetty-Nickel, *Luther and Culture,* 169.
24. *Hymni Lutheri animos plures, quam scripta et declamationes occiderunt* (1620), cited by Koch, vol. I, 244; quoted by Hoetty-Nickel, *Luther and Culture,* 170.
25. *Thesaurus Sapientiae,* Book VIII, Part II (Antwerp, 1603), 41; cited by Hoetty-Nickel, *Luther and Culture,* 170.
26. Nettl, *Luther and Music,* 29.
27. Robert M. Stevenson, *Patterns of Protestant Church Worship* (Durham, N.C.: Duke University Press, 1953), 3.
28. John Calvin, *Homiliae in primum librum Samuelis* (Geneva, Switzerland: 1604), 370; quoted by Stevenson, *Patterns of Protestant Church Worship,* 13-14.
29. Breed, *History and Use of Hymns,* 290.
30. *Ibid.,* 22, 54.
31. H. A. L. Jefferson, *Hymns in Christian Worship* (New York: The Macmillian Company, 1950), 33.
32. Jefferson, *Hymns in Christian Worship,* 34.

33. Donald P. Hustad, *Jubilate! Church Music in the Evangelical Tradition* (Carol Stream, Ill.: Hope, 1981), 134.
34. Breed, *History and Use of Hymns*, 301-303.
35. Stevenson, *Patterns of Protestant Church Worship*, 17-18.
36. *Ibid.*, 302-303.

CHAPTER 10. FROM PSALM SINGING TO HYMNODY

1. Paul Davis, *Isaac Watts: His Life and Works* (New York: Dryden, 1943), 188-189.
2. Davis, *Isaac Watts*, 188-189.
3. Donald D. Hustad, *Jubilate! Church Music in the Evangelical Tradition* (Carol Stream, Ill.: Hope, 1981), 245.
4. Davis, *Isaac Watts*, 158, 159, 196, 197.
5. *Ibid.*, 19.
6. Arthur L. Rich, *World Book Encyclopedia*, vol. 21 (Chicago: Worldbook-Childcraft International, Inc., 1978), 119. Over six hundred of these were hymns (Davis, *Isaac Watts*, 212).
7. Davis, *Isaac Watts*, 202-203.
8. *Ibid.*, 197.
9. Preface to *Horae Lyricae* (2nd ed., 1709); cited in Davis, *Isaac Watts*, 159.
10. Davis, *Isaac Watts*, 159.
11. *Ibid.*, 207.
12. William Romaine, *The Whole Works* (London, 1787), 990; cited by Stevenson, *Patterns of Protestant Church Worship* (Durham, N.C.: Duke University Press, 1953), 95.

13. Romaine, *The Whole Works,* 999.
14. H. A. L. Jefferson, *Hymns in Christian Worship* (New York: Macmillian, 1950), 1-2.
15. Millar Patrick, *The Story of the Church's Song* (Richmond, Va.: John Knox Press, 1962), 124.
16. Stevenson, *Patterns of Protestant Church Worship,* 99.
17. *Ibid.,* 105-106.
18. Patrick, *The Story of the Church's Song,* 128.
19. Stevenson, *Patterns of Protestant Church Worship,* 116.
20. *Ibid.,* 133.
21. James Sallee, *A History of Evangelistic Hymnody* (Grand Rapids, Mich.: Baker Book House, 1978), 14.
22. Sallee, *History of Evangelistic Hymnody,* 26.
23. Harold Myra and Dean Merrill, *Rock, Bach, and Superschlock* (Philadelphia: J. B. Lippincott, 1972), 93; quoted in Donald Paul Ellsworth, *Christian Music in Contemporary Witness* (Grand Rapids, Mich.: Baker Book House, 1979), 73.
24. Leonard J. Seidel, *Face the Music: Contemporary Church Music on Trial* (Springfield, Va.: Grace Unlimited Publications, 1988), 137-138.
25. Sallee, *History of Evangelistic Hymnody,* 131.
26. Ellsworth, *Christian Music in Contemporary Witness,* 75.
27. Arnold A. Dallimore, *A Heart Set Free: The Life of Charles Wesley* (Wheaton, Ill.: Crossway Books, 1988), 215.

28. Sallee, *History of Evangelistic Hymnody*, 19-20.
29. *Ibid.*, 23.
30. Joshua Leavitt, *The Christian Lyre* (1831); cited by Henry Wilder Foote, *Three Centuries of American Hymnody* (Cambridge: Harvard University Press, 1940), 203; quoted by Sallee, *A History of Evangelistic Hymnody*, 45.
31. Sallee, *History of Evangelistic Hymnody*, 26.
32. *Ibid.*, 31-32.
33. Ellsworth, *Christian Music in Contemporary Witness*, 86.
34. Faith Coxe Bailey, *D. L. Moody: The Greatest Evangelist of the Nineteenth Century* (Chicago: Moody, 1959), 120.
35. J. C. Pollock, *Moody: A Biographical Portrait of the Pacesetter in Modern Mass Evangelism* (New York: The Macmillan Company, 1963), 95.
36. T. H. Hall, *Biography of Gospel Song and Hymn Writers* (New York: AMS Press, 1971), 198-199; quoted in Sallee, *History of Evangelistic Hymnody*, 58.
37. Sallee, *History of Evangelistic Hymnody*, 58.
38. Stevenson, *Patterns of Protestant Church Worship*, 153.
39. Pollock, *Moody: A Biographical Portrait*, 137.
40. *Ibid.*, 135.
41. Rufus W. Clark, *The Work of God in Great Britain Under Mssrs. Moody and Sankey* (New York: Harper and Brothers, 1875), 148.
42. Sallee, *History of Evangelistic Hymnody*, 63.
43. *Ibid.*, 63

44. Pollock, *Moody: A Biographical Portrait,* 134.
45. *Ibid.,* 136.
46. *Ibid.,* 119.
47. Henry Davenport Northrop, *Life and Labors of Dwight L. Moody* (Philadelphia: National, 1899), 94.
48. Bailey, *D. L. Moody: The Greatest Evangelist,* 107.
49. *Ibid.,* 107
50. Ira D. Sankey, *My Life and the Story of the Gospel Hymns* (New York: Harper and Brothers, 1907), 62, 64.
51. Barnard Watson, *A Hundred Years' War: The Salvation Army: 1865–1965* (Hodder and Stoughton), 85.
52. Robert Sandall, *The History of the Salvation Army,* vol. II (Nashville: Thomas Nelson, 1950), 102.
53. Sandall, *History of the Salvation Army,* 102.
54. Watson, *A Hundred Years' War,* 86.
55. *Ibid.,* 89.
56. *Ibid.,* 91.
57. *Ibid.,* 83.
58. *Ibid.,* 89.
59. Sandall, *History of the Salvation Army,* 110.
60. *Ibid.,* 106-107.
61. *Ibid.,* 200.
62. Watson, *A Hundred Years' War,* 83.
63. Sandall, *History of the Salvation Army,* vol. II, 111.
64. *Ibid.,* vol. I, 210.
65. *Ibid.,* 112.

CHAPTER 11. WHAT WE CAN LEARN FROM HISTORY

1. Georg Wilhelm Friedrich Hegel, *The Philosophy of History,* translated by J. Sibree (New York: Dover Publications, Inc., 1956), 6.
2. F. E. Kirby, *A Short History of Keyboard Music* (New York: The Free Press, 1966), 5.
3. Donald P. Hustad, *Jubilate! Church Music in the Evangelical Tradition* (Carol Stream, Ill.: Hope, 1981), 275-276.
4. Edwin Liemohn, *The Organ and Choir in Protestant Worship* (Philadelphia: Fortress, 1968), 4.
5. Liemohn, *The Organ and Choir in Protestant Worship,* 2.
6. Robert M. Stevenson, *Patterns of Protestant Church Music* (Duke University Press: 1953), 3.
7. Stevenson, *Patterns of Protestant Church Music,* 3.
8. *Ibid.,* 17-18.
9. *Ibid.,* 17-18.
10. Edward S. Ninde, *The Story of the American Hymn* (Nashville, Tenn.: Abingdon, 1921), 94-95.
11. Ninde, *Story of the American Hymn,* 96, 97.
12. Dan Peters, Steve Peters, and Cher Merrill, *What about Christian Rock?* (Minneapolis, Minn.: Bethany House, 1986), 196.
13. Don Wyrtzen and Dave Wyrtzen, "The Beat Debate," *Moody Monthly* (Sept. 1985), 33.
14. Gordon L. Borror and Ronald B. Allen, *Worship: Rediscovering the Missing Jewel* (Portland, Oreg.: Multnomah, 1982), 167.

15. Borror and Allen, *Worship: Rediscovering the Missing Jewel,* 34.
16. Hustad, *Jubilate!* 275-277.
17. *Ibid.,* 288.
18. *Ibid.,* 311.
19. *Ibid.,* 46-47.
20. Compare Hustad, *Jubilate!* 35, 127, for a similar evaluation.
21. J. I. Packer, "All That Jazz," *Christianity Today* (12 Dec. 1986), 15.
22. Millar Patrick, *The Story of the Church's Song* (Richmond, Va.: John Knox, 1962), 135.
23. W. C. Proctor, *The Story of the Church's Song* (London: James Clarke, n.d.), 57.
24. Hustad, *Jubilate!* 202. See also Donald Paul Ellsworth: "Each time the church has expressed its beliefs in a contemporary way it has surged forward in evangelistic outreach, bringing scores of people into the church." *Christian Music in Contemporary Witness* (Grand Rapids, Mich.: Baker Book House, 1979), 18.
25. Sankey, *My Life and the Story of the Gospel Hymns,* 62.

Chapter 12. The Need for an Alternative

1. Allan Bloom, *The Closing of the American Mind* (New York: Simon and Schuster, 1987), 68.
2. Bob Macken, Peter Fornatale, and Bill Ayres, *The Rock Music Source Book* (New York: Anchor, 1980), 15.
3. Elizabeth F. Brown and William R. Hendee,

"Adolescents and Their Music," *Journal of the American Medical Association* 262:12 (22–29 Sept. 1989), 1659.

4. Peggy Mann, "How Shock Rock Harms Our Kids," *Reader's Digest* (July 1988), 102.

5. Dan Peters, Steve Peters, and Cher Merrill, *What about Christian Rock?* (Minneapolis, Minn.: Bethany House, 1986), 19.

6. Tony Clifton, "The Sexy Godmother of Rock," *Newsweek* (4 Mar. 1985).

7. Maureen Orth, "The Sunshine Boy," *Newsweek* (20 Dec. 1976), 66.

8. Orth, "Sunshine Boy," 68.

9. Jacob Aranza, *Backward Masking Unmasked* (Shreveport, La.: Huntington House, 1980), 59; quoting *Hit Parader* (July 1975), 64.

10. Barry L. Sherman and Joseph R. Dominick, "Violence and Sex in Music Videos: TV and Rock'n'Roll," *Journal of Communication* 36 (Winter 1986), 79-93.

11. Edward G. Armstrong, "Country Music Sex Songs: An Ethnomusicological Account," *The Journal of Sex Research* 22:3 (Aug. 1986), 371.

12. Armstrong, "Country Music Sex Songs," 372.

13. Al Menconi, *Today's Music: A Window to Your Child's Soul* (Elgin, Ill.: David C. Cook, 1990), 93.

14. *People* (19 Nov. 1984), 161ff.

15. Eric Holmberg, *Hell's Bells: The Dangers of Rock and Roll,* manuscript of video series, 17.

16. Peters, Peters, and Merrill, *What about Christian Rock?* 24; quoting *Star Hits* (Sept. 1985).

17. *Rolling Stone* (28 Feb. 1985), 16.
18. Ben Liemer, "W.A.S.P.'s Metal Venom," *Circus* (28 Feb. 1985), 102.
19. Richard Hogan, "Ratt: Undercover Agents," *Hit Parader*, 46.
20. Holmburg, *Hell's Bells*, 14; quoting Bob DeMoss, Jr., "Rising to the Challenge" (Vision Video, Parents Music Resource Center, 1988).
21. Michael K. Haynes, *The God of Rock* (Lindale, Tex.: Priority Ministries and Publications, 1982), 172.
22. Peters, Peters, and Merrill, *What about Christian Rock?* 21.
23. Kane, *Misogyny in Rock Videos* (New York: Women Against Pornography, 1984); quoted by Dena L. Peterson and Karen S. Pfost, "Influence of Rock Videos on Attitudes of Violence against Women," *Psychological Reports* (1989), 319.
24. *Newsweek* (6 Nov. 1967), 101; quoted by Haynes, *The God of Rock*, 174.
25. *Hit Parader*, 49.
26. "Motley Crue: The Road Warriors," *Hit Parader's Heavy Metal Heroes* (Mar. 1985), 9.
27. *Life* (3 Oct. 1969), 4; quoted by Haynes, *The God of Rock*, 198.
28. Haynes, *The God of Rock*, 198.
29. *Ibid.*, 195.
30. Peters, Peters, and Merrill, *What about Christian Rock?* 105.

CHAPTER 13. COMMUNICATING MUSICAL CONVICTIONS TO YOUR CHILDREN

1. Al Menconi, "Whose Records Should I Burn? Alice's or Amy's?" *Media Update* 6:3 (May/June 1987).
2. Al Menconi, *Today's Music: A Window to Your Child's Soul* (Elgin, Ill.: David C. Cook, 1990), back book sleeve.
3. Dena L. Peterson and Karen S. Pfost, "Influence of Rock Videos on Attitudes of Violence Against Women," *Psychological Reports* 64 (1989), 321.
4. Peggy Mann, "How Shock Rock Harms Our Kids," *Reader's Digest* (July 1988), 103.
5. L. E. Greeson and R. A. Williams, "Social Implications of Music Videos for Youth: An Analysis of the Contents and Affects of MTV," *Youth and Society* 18 (1986), 177-189.
6. It would be quite difficult to design a study that could prove these long-term effects. Brown and Hendee of the American Medical Association summarize the present state of psychological studies: "Current evidence suggests only that this music [secular heavy metal groups such as Slayer] could possibly promote destructive behavior in certain susceptible individuals who are already alienated from mainstream society." Elizabeth Brown and William R. Hendee, *Journal of the American Medical Association* 263:6 (9 Feb. 1990), 812, clarifying their position presented in "Adolescents and Their Music," *Journal of the American Medical Association* 202:12 (22–29

Sept. 1989), 1659-1663. More extensive studies documenting the negative impact of pornography should warn us of the potential impact of violent and sexually explicit music. For studies on the negative influence of pornography, see Tom Minnery, ed., *Pornography: A Human Tragedy* (Wheaton, Ill.: Tyndale House, 1986), 115-161.

7. Richard Francis Weymouth, *Weymouth's New Testament in Modern Speech,* revised by J. A. Robertson, (London: James Clarke and Company, Ltd.).

8. Kristine McKenna, "Sting: The Rolling Stone Interview," *Rolling Stone* (September 1983).

9. Dan Peters and Steve Peters, *Why Knock Rock?* (Minneapolis, Minn.: Bethany House, 1984), 81.

10. *Rock!* (Feb. 1985), 27.

11. Peters and Peters, *Why Knock Rock?* 121.

12. *Ibid.,* 123.

13. *Ibid.,* 131.

14. *Ibid.,* 132.

CHAPTER 14. A CHRISTIAN ALTERNATIVE

1. Al Menconi, *Today's Music: A Window to Your Child's Soul* (Elgin, Ill.: David C. Cook, 1990), 152.

2. John W. Still, "It's Time for a New Revolution," *Contemporary Christian Music* (Jan. 1991), 24.

3. Allen Weed, "Music in Your Ministry," *Network News* 8:4 (Fall 1990), 3.

4. Donald P. Hustad, *Jubilate! Church Music in the Evangelical Tradition* (Carol Stream, Ill.: Hope, 1981), 165.

5. *Today's Teens: A Generation in Transition* (Glendale, Calif.: The Barna Research Group, 1991), 29.

6. *Today's Teens*, 29.

7. "Echoes" newsletter (Waco, Tex.: Word, Inc.), 5.

8. *Ibid.*, 5. For further background on Petra, see *War and Remembrance*, booklet enclosed with tape set of same name. See also *Contemporary Christian Music* (Jan. 1982), 13.

9. *War and Remembrance*.

10. Warren Anderson, "Beyond Rock," *Contemporary Christian Music* (June 1990), 34.

11. "Five Minutes with Josh" (monthly newsletter of the Josh McDowell Ministry of Campus Crusade for Christ International, Dallas, Tex.).

12. "Echoes" newsletter.

13. "An Evening with Keith Green" concert brochure.

14. Melody Green and David Hazard, *No Compromise: The Life Story of Keith Green* (Chatsworth, Calif.: Sparrow Press, 1989), 291.

15. Frank Garlock, *Can Rock Music Be Sacred?* 35.

16. Quincy Smith-Newcomb, "Rez Band—Chicago Band Makes Music Loving Their Neighbors," *Contemporary Christian Music* (Feb. 1984), 16-19.

17. Smith-Newcomb, "Rez Band," 16-19.

18. "Broken Heart News," (newsletter of Broken Heart Ministries), 6.

19. *Ibid.*, 2.

20. Jerry Wilson, "Rock Evangelist for the 90s," *Contemporary Christian Music* (July 1990), 30.
21. Wilson, "Rock Evangelist for the 90s," 32.

CHAPTER 15. TAKING IT TO THE CHURCH

1. *Newsweek* (30 Dec. 1985), 54; quoted by Dan Peters, Steve Peters, and Cher Merrill, *What about Christian Rock?* (Minneapolis, Minn.: Bethany House, 1986), 21.
2. Frank R. Tillapaugh, *The Church Unleashed* (Ventura, Calif.: Regal, 1982).
3. Donald P. Hustad, "Must the Aucas Sing Our Songs?" *Eternity* (Feb. 1967), 51-52, 54.
4. See Delbert Rice, "Developing an Indigenous Hymnody," *Practical Anthropology* (May/June, 1971), 112.
5. R. LaVerne Morse, "Ethnomusicology: A New Frontier," *Evangelical Missions Quarterly* 11:1 (January 1975), 33.
6. Morse, "Ethnomusicology: A New Frontier," 35. Along this line, the Loma people of Liberia were exposed to classical pieces that expressed distinct emotions to Westerners. None of these emotions came through to the Loma. Apparently, no one style of music is a universal language. Alan P. Merriam, *The Anthropology of Music* (Evanston, Ill.: Northwestern University Press, 1964), 11-12.
7. Hustad, "Must the Aucas Sing Our Songs?" 51-52, 54. See also Darrell A. Mock, "Christian Music in Japan," *The Church Musician* 29 (Aug. 1978), 12-13: "Translating Western poetry into

meaningful Japanese is next to impossible when
setting the words to Western hymn tunes."

8. Albert W. D. Frieson, "A Methodology in the
   Development of Indigenous Hymnody,"
   Missiology: An International Review 10:1 (Jan.
   1982), 83.

9. T. W. Hunt, *Music in Missions: Discipling
   through Music* (Nashville, Tenn.: Broadman,
   1987), 113. See also Vida Chenoweth and
   Darlene Bee, "On Ethnic Music," *Practical
   Anthropology* (Sept.–Oct. 1978), 207: "Like any
   language, music must be domestic to be
   understood. Christianity expressed in the
   language of a people strikes home. Christianity
   expressed in the musical idiom of a people
   reinforces the spoken message at the greatest
   depth."

10. Hunt, *Music in Missions*, 123.

11. *Ibid.*, 16.

12. *Ibid.*, 16.

13. *Ibid.*, 22.

14. *Ibid.*, 88.

15. Bill O'Brien and Dellanna O'Brien, "Building an
    Indigenous Music Program in Indonesia," *The
    Church Musician* (July 1972), 4.

16. Hunt, *Music in Missions*, 128-129.

17. Rice, "Developing an Indigenous Hymnody,"
    111-112.

18. Ronald Zalkind, *Contemporary Music Almanac:
    1980–1981* (Schirmer Books, 1980), 80-81.

19. See Chenoweth and Bee, "On Ethnic Music,"

209. "A non-Christian society has concepts and practices that are in violent opposition to those of Christian society. These are expressed both in its language and in its music. However, these vehicles of expression are themselves without moral quality and are able to accommodate new concepts and to eliminate old ones."

20. L. P. Hartley, *The Go-Between* (New York: Alfred Knopf, 1953).

21. Gordon L. Borror and Ronald B. Allen, *Worship: Rediscovering the Missing Jewel* (Portland, Oreg.: Multnomah, 1982), 166.

22. J. David Stone, *Youthworker* (Spring 1990), 45.

23. Al Menconi, *Today's Music: A Window to Your Child's Soul* (Elgin, Ill.: David C. Cook, 1990), 128.

24. "Gospel Music Rolls Out of the Church, Onto the Charts," *U.S. News and World Report* (25 Aug. 1986), 56.

25. *God's Lively People* (Huntington, N.Y.: Fontana, 1971), 206; quoted by John R. W. Stott, *Christian Mission in a Modern World* (Downer's Grove, Ill.: InterVarsity Press, 1975), 122-123.

26. Doug Murren, *The Baby Boomerang* (Ventura, Calif.: Regal Books, 1990), 188. For those serious about reaching baby boomers, Murren's chapter on music should be thoroughly digested.

27. Reed Arvin, "Christian Music in a Post-Christian Culture," *Contemporary Christian Music* (Aug. 1990), 14.

CHAPTER 16. TAKING IT TO THE WORLD

1. Quoted by Ginger Sattler, "Scott Wesley Brown—I Want What I Do to Count," *Dove Club Newsletter* (Spring 1986), 1-2.

2. Donald P. Hustad, *Jubilate! Church Music in the Evangelical Tradition* (Carol Stream, Ill.: Hope, 1981), 4.

3. "The Forty Highest Paid Entertainers," *Atlanta Journal* (9 Sept. 1990), A-4.

4. Toby Creswell, "Jagger Scores Down Under," *Rolling Stone* (5 May 1988), 17.

5. Keith Cahoon, "Jagger Tour Rolls in Japan," *Rolling Stone* (5 May 1988), 17.

6. "All 'Bad' Things Come to an End as a Tearful Michael Jackson Bids Bye-Bye to the Highway," *People Weekly*, vol. 31, issue 6, (13 February 1989).

7. "Michael Jackson Says His 18-Month Worldwide Tour Was An 'Incredible Journey," *Jet*, (23 January 1989), 61.

8. Sam Emerson, "And in Ethiopia, the Cult of the Beloved One," *Newsweek* (25 May 1987), 31.

9. Paul Borthwick, "The Global Challenge of Youth Ministry," *Network News* 10(San Diego: National Network of Youth Ministries, Winter 1992), 1-2. Regarding the global village of teenagers, Daniel Offer, Eric Ostrov, Kenneth Howard, and Robert Atkinson studied about six thousand adolescents from ten diverse countries and noted that "a fourteen-year-old in Bangladesh may watch

the same television program as a fourteen-year-old in West Germany, Israel, Japan, Turkey, or Taiwan. Media knows no borders; ideas and events are transmitted to all corners of the globe, defining what is new or desirable, and are assimilated by young minds." *The Teenage World* (New York and London: Plenum Medical Book Company, 1988), 115.

10. Bob Hitching, "Michael Jackson vs. Mohammed," *Indeed* 3:2 (Operation Mobilization, April/May 1992), 1.

11. Fritz Rienecker and Cleon Rogers, *Linguistic Key to the Greek New Testament,* translated from *Sprachlicher Schluessel zum Griechischen Neun Testament,* edited by Cleon L. Rogers, Jr. (Grand Rapids, Mich.: Zondervan, 1976), 511.

12. J. B. Lightfoot, *The Epistle of St. Paul to the Galatians* (Grand Rapids, Mich.: Zondervan, 1957), 167-168.

13. H. A. Ironside, *Expository Messages on the Epistle to the Galatians* (Neptune, N.J.: Loizeaux Brothers, 1941), 136-137.

14. Donald K. Campbell, *The Bible Knowledge Commentary,* edited by John F. Walvoord and Roy B. Zuck (Wheaton, Ill.: Victor Books, 1978), 601.

15. Merrill C. Tenney, *New Testament Survey* (Grand Rapids, Mich.: Eerdmans, 1961), 1, 19, 61, 80, 117.

16. Dave Geisler, "Musicianaries for Christ," *Contemporary Christian Music* (May 1990), 26.

17. "Rocking the Soviet Corners," *Contemporary Christian Music* (Sept. 1990), 13.

18. "Rockingthe Soviet Corners," 13.

19. Personal interview with Danny Layman (Fall 1990).

20. Geisler, "Musicianaries for Christ," 22-23.

21. Sattler, "Scott Wesley Brown," 1-2.

22. Personal interview with George Verwer (Winter 1991).

23. Geisler, "Musicianaries for Christ," 23, 26, 28.

24. William MacDonald, *True Discipleship* (Kansas City, Kan.: Walterick, 1975), 31.

25. Steve Haggerty, "On the Road for God," *Charisma* (Nov. 1985); quoted in Dan Peters, Steve Peters, and Cher Merrill, *What about Christian Rock?* (Minneapolis, Minn.: Bethany House, 1986).

APPENDIX

HOW FOUR GROWING CHURCHES USE CONTEMPORARY MUSIC

1. Sources for Second Baptist Church: personal interviews; Elmer L. Towns, *An Inside Look at Ten of Today's Most Innovative Churches,* (Ventura, Calif.: Regal, 1990).

2. Sources for Eastside Foursquare Church: personal interviews; Doug Murren, *The Baby Boomerang,* (Ventura, Calif.: Regal, 1990).

3. Murren, *The Baby Boomerang,* 199.

4. Sources for Willow Creek Community Church: personal interviews; "Worship for the Believer" and "Foundations of a Music Ministry," tapes

from Willow Creek's Church Leadership
Conference; Towns, *An Inside Look.*
5. Sources for Mount Paran Church of God:
personal interviews; Towns, *An Inside Look.*